5™

500

AP World History: Modern Questions

to know by test day

7/20

D1496223

5 Steps to a 5: AP World History: Modern
5 Steps to a 5: AP World History: Modern Elite Student Edition

Also in the 500 AP Questions to Know by Test Day Series:
5 Steps to a 5: 500 AP Biology Questions to Know by Test Day, Third Edition
5 Steps to a 5: 500 AP Calculus AB/BC Questions to Know by Test Day, Third Edition
5 Steps to a 5: 500 AP Chemistry Questions to Know by Test Day, Third Edition
5 Steps to a 5: 500 AP English Literature Questions to Know by Test Day, Third Edition
5 Steps to a 5: 500 AP English Language Questions to Know by Test Day, Second Edition
5 Steps to a 5: 500 AP Environmental Science Questions to Know by Test Day, Second Edition
5 Steps to a 5: 500 AP European History Questions to Know by Test Day, Third Edition
5 Steps to a 5: 500 AP Human Geography to Know by Test Day, Third Edition
5 Steps to a 5: 500 AP Microeconomics Questions to Know by Test Day, Second Edition
5 Steps to a 5: 500 AP Macroeconomics Questions to Know by Test Day, Second Edition
5 Steps to a 5: 500 AP Physics 1 Questions to Know by Test Day, Third Edition
5 Steps to a 5: 500 AP Physics C Questions to Know by Test Day
5 Steps to a 5: 500 AP Psychology Questions to Know by Test Day, Third Edition
5 Steps to a 5: 500 AP Statistics Questions to Know by Test Day, Third Edition
5 Steps to a 5: 500 AP U.S. Government & Politics Questions to Know by Test Day, Third Edition
5 Steps to a 5: 500 AP U.S. History Questions to Know by Test Day, Third Edition

5 STEPS TO A >5™

500

AP World History: Modern
Questions

to know by test day

THIRD EDITION

Sean McManamon

New York Chicago San Francisco Athens London Madrid
Mexico City Milan New Delhi Singapore Sydney Toronto

1 2 3 4 5 6 7 8 9   LCR   25 24 23 22 21 20

ISBN   978-1-260-46019-3
MHID   1-260-46019-3

e-ISBN   978-1-260-46020-9
e-MHID   1-260-46020-7

Contributions from former editions by Adam Stevens.

McGraw-Hill Education products are available at special quantity discounts to use as premiums and sales promotions or for use in corporate training programs. To contact a representative, please visit the Contact Us pages at www.mhprofessional.com.

CONTENTS

ABOUT THE AUTHOR

Sean McManamon has a Masters in History from Hunter College, 1998. He teaches AP World History at Brooklyn Technical High School and lives in Manhattan with his wife, Justine, and two children, Phebe and Owen.

INTRODUCTION

Congratulations! You've taken a big step toward AP success by purchasing *5 Steps to a 5: 500 AP World History Modern Questions to Know by Test Day.* We are here to help you take the next step and score high on your AP Exam so you can earn college credits and get into the college or university of your choice!

This book gives you 500 AP-style multiple-choice questions that cover all the most essential course material. Each question has a detailed answer explanation. These questions will give you valuable independent practice to supplement your regular textbook and the groundwork you are already doing in your AP classroom.

Each chapter ends with a set of stimulus-based questions of the type the College Board has recently employed in its redesigned AP World History exam. As you complete these questions use a timer, and work toward completing each stimulus-based question in one minute or less. Working at this speed will prepare you for the pace you will want to maintain when taking the actual AP exam in the spring.

This and the other books in this series were written by expert AP teachers who know your exam inside out and can identify the crucial exam information as well as questions that are most likely to appear on the exam.

You might be the kind of student who takes several AP courses and needs to study extra questions throughout the year. Or you might be the kind of student who puts off preparing until the last weeks before the exam. No matter what your preparation style, you will surely benefit from reviewing these 500 questions, which closely parallel the content, format, and degree of difficulty of the questions on the actual AP exam. These questions and their answer explanations are the ideal last-minute study tool for those final few weeks before the test.

Remember the old saying "Practice makes perfect." If you practice with all the questions and answers in this book, we are certain you will build the skills and confidence needed to do well on the exam. Good luck!

—Editors of McGraw-Hill Education

5 STEPS TO A 5

500

AP World History: Modern Questions

to know by test day

CHAPTER 1

The Postclassical Era: 1200 CE to 1450

Controlling Idea: Resurgence

As we approach the history of the world in the year 1200, we see a global tapestry: a wide variety of peoples, states, and lands, in different levels of contact with one another. This unit is the story of a regeneration of centralized political authority that first matches and then surpasses levels of imperial cohesion seen in the era of classical civilizations. By 1200, previously nomadic peoples have expanded, settled down, and established states. We also notice that by 1200 the major world religions are established, roughly, in the areas they hold sway until today. By 1450 a Resurgence has been completed, and broadly speaking each center of civilization has recovered, consolidated, and expanded upon earlier glories. The great outlier when speaking in such general terms are the civilizations of the Americas, which, while developing along familiar lines seen elsewhere in earlier eras, are not integrated into global networks of long distance trade by 1450.

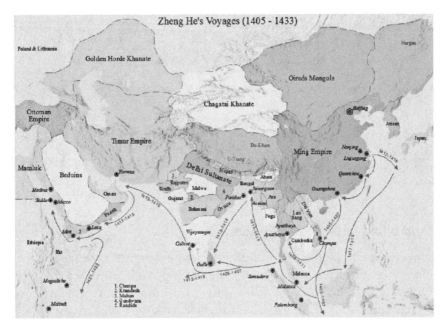

—Map showing Asian continent

1. Which of the following best explains a historical argument on why the Chinese abandoned the commercial voyages of the Zheng He expeditions?

   (A) The trade with foreign regions was seen as unnecessary and costly with little reward for China.

   (B) The size of the fleets was so limited that they could not compete with the greater capacity of the Europeans.

   (C) Chinese navigational skills were inadequate to expand areas of expedition beyond the Pacific Ocean.

   (D) There was little of value for the Chinese to export, and the voyages were expensive to carry out.

2. China's Treasure Fleet voyages by Admiral Zheng He reached as far west as which of the following areas?

   (A) The Horn of Africa

   (B) The Straits of Hormuz

   (C) The Khyber Pass

   (D) The Straits of Malacca

Name of Chinese Civilizations	Dates of Rule
Song	960–1279
Yuan	1271–1368
Ming	1368–1644
Qing	1644–1911

3. The different Chinese civilizations above are most commonly defined as which of the following?
   (A) Feudalists
   (B) Monarchies
   (C) Dynasties
   (D) Shogunates

4. Which of the following philosophical innovations did traditional China develop to explain the change in ruling governments?
   (A) Sinification
   (B) Mandate of Heaven
   (C) Three Perfections
   (D) Filial piety

—Detail of a scroll painting, "Along the River During the Qingming Festival" by Zhang Zeduan.

5. The image above best supports which of the following conclusions about Song dynasty China?

   (A) The Mongol invasions devastated most Chinese cities.
   (B) There was vibrant and bustling trade in China's cities.
   (C) Buddhist beliefs spread from Central Asia.
   (D) Peasants began to migrate to Northern China.

6. Which group in Chinese society was ranked the lowest according to Confucian teachings?

   (A) Peasants
   (B) Craft workers
   (C) Merchants
   (D) Scholars

—Chinese mosque in the city of Xi'an.

7. Which of the following conclusions is best supported by the photo of an Islamic mosque with Arabic writing in the Chinese city of X'ian?

   (A) Islam blended with some aspects of Chinese culture.
   (B) Islamic writing was adopted by the Chinese government.
   (C) Islam spread West from China to the Middle East.
   (D) Chinese culture was strictly ethnocentric when it came to all outside influences.

8. Which of the following conclusions is best supported by the photo of a mosque in the Chinese city of Xi'an?

   (A) China rejected Islam within its borders during the Postclassical Era.
   (B) Islam came to China during the Preclassical Era.
   (C) Islam reached China during the Postclassical Era.
   (D) China adopted Islam as the state religion during the Modern Era.

Your servant begs leave to say that Buddhism is no more than a cult of the barbarian peoples, which spread to China in the time of the Latter Han. It did not exist here in ancient times . . . When Emperor Gaozu received the throne from the House of Sui, he deliberated upon the suppression of Buddhism. But at that time the various officials, being of small worth and knowledge, were unable fully to comprehend the ways of the ancient kings and the exigencies of past and present, and so could not implement the wisdom of the emperor and rescue the age from corruption. Thus the matter came to naught, to your servant's constant regret. . . . Now Buddha was a man of the barbarians who did not speak the language of China and wore clothes of a different fashion. His sayings did not concern the ways of our ancient kings, nor did his manner of dress conform to their laws. He understood neither the duties that bind sovereign and subject nor the affections of father and son.

—Postclassical account on Buddhism in China.

9. The attitudes above were most commonly expressed by which of the following people in traditional Chinese society?
   (A) Wandering Daoists
   (B) Muslim traders
   (C) Confucian scholars
   (D) Buddhist monks

10. Which of the following best describes the author's attitude?
    (A) Ethnocentric
    (B) Interdependent
    (C) Missionary
    (D) Warlike

11. Which statement comparing Postclassical Chinese civilization with contemporary Western civilization is most accurate?
    (A) The Chinese economy relied on slavery to a greater extent than Western civilization did.
    (B) China set an enduring pattern of more sophisticated agricultural, metallurgical, and textile production techniques than Western civilization.
    (C) Women had markedly greater maneuverability within Chinese civilization to achieve positions of high social status.
    (D) The Chinese developed a simplified phonetic writing system similar to Hebrew.

12. Which is most true about the staffing of the central administration of the Imperial bureaucracy in the Tang-Song era?

    (A) Administrators were selected based on civil service exams
    (B) Positions were dominated by sinicized nomads.
    (C) Administrators were selected by the emperor.
    (D) The staff comprised individuals from prominent families.

13. Which group benefited from newfound higher status in the period of Mongol rule in China?

    (A) Scholar-gentry
    (B) Aristocracy
    (C) Peasantry
    (D) Merchants

14. Which is not a native Chinese invention?

    (A) Explosive gun powder
    (B) Magnetic compass
    (C) Movable type
    (D) Steam-powered machinery

15. Which practice dates from the Postclassical Era in China?

    (A) Foot-binding
    (B) Arranged marriage
    (C) Concubinage
    (D) Divorce rights

—Buddhist Temple in Kyoto, Japan

16. The above image proves which of the following statements?
    (A) Indian Hinduism was popular in Japan.
    (B) China exerted a strong influence on Japan.
    (C) Buddhism was rejected by most Japanese.
    (D) Islam was adopted by the Japanese court.

17. Which of the following was another area that practiced a form of Buddhism similar to that in Japan?
    (A) The Philippines
    (B) Polynesia
    (C) Korea
    (D) Pakistan

... [Daimyo] *Yorimasa summoned* [samurai] *Watanabe Chûjitsu Tonau and ordered: "Strike off my head." Tonau could not bring himself to do this while his master was still alive. He wept bitterly. "How can I do that, my lord?" he replied. "I can do so only after you have committed suicide." "I understand," said Yorimasa. He turned to the west, joined his palms, and chanted "Hail Amidha Buddha" ten times in a loud voice. Then he composed this poem:*

Like a fossil tree

Which has borne not one blossom

Sad has been my life

Sadder still to end my days

Leaving no fruit behind me.

Having spoken these lines, he thrust the point of his sword into his belly, bowed his face to the ground as the blade pierce him through, and died. ... Tonau took up his master's head and, weeping, fastened it to a stone. Then, evading the enemy, he made his way to the river and sank it in a deep place.

—Excerpts from *The Tale of the Heike*, late 12th century

18. The prevalence of samurai and feudal lords demonstrates which of the following historical facts about Postclassical Japan?
    (A) Japan's lack of a common culture and language
    (B) Japan's lack of political unity and government
    (C) Japan's lack of belief systems and religions
    (D) Japan's lack of access to water-based trade

19. Which of the following warrior codes was followed by the Japanese samurai?
    (A) Bushido
    (B) Kamikaze
    (C) Zen
    (D) Kamakura

—Images from a Japanese scroll showing the Mongol Invasion of Japan in 1274.

20. Which of the following was a result of the Mongol invasion of Japan in 1274?

(A) It succeeded in partitioning the country into Mongol tribute states.

(B) It failed due to fierce Japanese resistance and ocean storms.

(C) It was derailed due to the death of Genghis Khan in Mongolia.

(D) It was followed by the Mongol invasion of Western Europe.

21. Which of the following feelings later developed in Japan due to the Mongol Invasions in the 13th century?

(A) Japanese desire to engage with the world

(B) Japanese ethnocentric and xenophobic ideas

(C) Japanese cultural missions to India and China

(D) Japanese embrace of China's warrior culture

22. Which contemporary society most closely mirrored feudal Japanese patterns of decentralized rule, an economy based on agricultural peasant labor, and emergence of a warrior elite following a distinct code of honor?

(A) Polynesian

(B) Inca

(C) Western European

(D) Russian

23. Postclassical Japan borrowed much from Chinese culture EXCEPT:

(A) writing system

(B) Confucianism

(C) Buddhism

(D) civil service exam

24. The Japanese emperor differs from the Chinese emperor in that

(A) He inherits his rule from a family member

(B) He has more power than a Chinese emperor

(C) He has little power and acts as a figurehead

(D) He belongs to scholar-gentry class

—Angkor Wat temple complex

25. The Angkor Wat Temple in Cambodia shows a strong cultural influence from which of the following regions?
    (A) Chinese
    (B) Persian
    (C) Roman
    (D) Indian

26. The Angkor Wat Temple shows the influence from which two belief systems?
    (A) Hinduism and Buddhism
    (B) Islam and Sikhism
    (C) Jainism and Hinduism
    (D) Confucian and Daoism

—Photo in Vietnam, 2010

27. The above image helps proves which of the following statements?
    (A) Buddhism promotes the monastic lifestyle for its followers.
    (B) Vietnamese men shaved their hair in respect for the Emperor.
    (C) Islamic identity is strong in northern Vietnam.
    (D) Confucian ethics are not promoted in Vietnam.

28. Which form of Buddhism was most influential in Vietnam?
    (A) Theravada
    (B) Mahayana
    (C) Zen
    (D) Shinto

29. Which of the following does NOT belong in a list of similarities in the process of how Islam spread to South Asia, Southeast Asia, and Africa?

    (A) Islam arrived with traders and took root first in urban areas.

    (B) The spread of Islam was mainly peaceful.

    (C) Political power remained in the hands of non-Arab elites.

    (D) A majority of the population in all three areas converted to Islam.

30. What was a common feature of Postclassical civilizations in India, China, and the Mediterranean?

    (A) Agricultural systems dependent on monsoon rains

    (B) Social hierarchy

    (C) Absence of coerced labor

    (D) Elimination of patriarchy over time

31. By the Postclassical Era, what similarity did Buddhism and Christianity share?

    (A) Support for caste hierarchy

    (B) Requirement of total celibacy for men

    (C) Allowance of women to enter monastic life

    (D) Inclusion of Greek and Roman gods into their pantheon

—Muslim scientists in *The House of Wisdom*

32. Based on the preceding image which of the following is true of Islamic Civilization by the time of the Abbasid empire?

    (A) They taught and tested Confucian values in their schools.
    (B) They achieved great advances in the sciences.
    (C) They expanded to rule over northern Europe.
    (D) They used a Sanskrit form of writing.

33. Which city became the capital of the Abbasid Empire and a center of what has been termed an Islamic golden age?

    (A) Istanbul
    (B) Timbuktu
    (C) Seville
    (D) Baghdad

—Sketch of a caravanserai in the Middle East

34. Which of the following was a continuity in the use of the caravanserai depicted above?

    (A) They provided food, lodging, and a place to conduct business along the western end of the Silk Road.

    (B) They were used as military strong points and fortifications by the Arabs against the European Crusaders.

    (C) They acted as centers of religious worship and helped to promote Nestorian Christianity and Judaism.

    (D) They were examples of monumental architecture to glorify the local elites and give patronage to artists.

35. Which of the following historical events helped diminish the use of the buildings shown on the previous page?

    (A) The seven treasure fleet voyages of the Chinese admiral Zheng He

    (B) The defeat of the Mongols over vast swaths of Eurasian territory

    (C) Vasco Da Gama's ships reaching India using an all-water route

    (D) The Viking Leif Erickson founding a settlement in Eastern Canada

News reached [Cairo and Syria] that the plague in Damascus had been less deadly than in Tripoli, Hama, and Aleppo. From . . . [October 1348] death raged with intensity. 1200 people died daily and, as a result, people stopped requesting permits from the administration to bury the dead and many cadavers were abandoned in gardens and on the roads. . . .

Family celebrations and marriages no longer took place. . . . No one held any festivities during the entire duration of the epidemic, and no voice was heard singing. . . . The call to prayer was suspended at many locations, and even at the most important ones, there remained only a single muezzin [caller to prayer]. . . .

Most of the mosques and zawiyas [Sufi lodges] were closed. . . .

The same thing happened throughout Egypt. When harvest time arrived, many farmers already perished [and no field hands remained to gather crops]. Soldiers and their young slaves or pages headed for the fields. They tried to recruit workers by promising them half of the proceeds, but they could not find anyone to gather the harvest. They threshed the grain with their horses [hoofs[, and winnowed the grain themselves, but, unable to carry all the grain back, they had to abandon much of it. . . .

Workers disappeared. You could not find either water carriers, or launderers or servants. The monthly salary of a horse groom rose from 30 to 80 dirhams. . . . This epidemic, they say, continued in several countries for 15 years.

—An Account of the Bubonic Plague in Syria and Egypt
by Ahmad al Maqrizi

36. Which of the following is true of the effects of the Black Death on the Middle East?
    (A) There were outbreaks of violence against Jews and other minorities.
    (B) There was an increase in the amount of people to act as a labor force.
    (C) There was an increase in the wages that laborers could command.
    (D) There was a prolonged decrease in trade in the Mediterranean Sea.

37. In comparison to the Black Death in Europe, the Mamluk Sultanate government's reaction to the crisis
    (A) Was similar in closing down public gatherings
    (B) Was different in the wages paid to laborers
    (C) Was in contrast to scapegoating the gypsies
    (D) Was the same in forcing soldiers into slavery

This terminology—ancient, medieval, modern—is not used almost universally, whether appropriate or not. Those of you who are students of Islam will certainly be aware of the famous book called "Medieval Islam" written by one of the most distinguished scholars in the field. It is an excellent book, but the title is an absurdity: what it means is not Medieval Islam—it means that period of Islamic history which corresponds to the Medieval period in European history. This classification—ancient, medieval, modern—is European; it was invented by Europeans to classify the different phases of European history; it was either adopted by or imposed upon the rest of the world, whether appropriate or not.

—From the historian, Bernard Lewis

38. The secondary source on historical writing above is best understood in the context of
    (A) Medievalism
    (B) Islamic exceptionalism
    (C) Eurocentrism
    (D) Globalization

39. In contrast with East Asia, the periodization of history there is divided into which of the following units for study?
    (A) Millenniums (1000 years)
    (B) Dynasties
    (C) Empires
    (D) Religions

40. According to the reasoning put forth in the reading, which historical change begins the era in the Middle East termed "Medieval"?
    (A) The birth of Jesus Christ
    (B) The fall of Rome
    (C) The rise of Islam
    (D) The European Crusades

41. Which of the following does NOT belong in a list of characteristics common to the decline of both the Byzantine and Abbasid empires?

(A) Chaotic succession fights for the imperial throne
(B) Frequent interference of military commanders in politics
(C) Growing dependence on nomadic warriors or mercenaries
(D) Imperial conversion to a new religion

42. Which intellectual or technological advancement CANNOT be traced to the era when Islamic civilization was at its height?

(A) Lateen sails
(B) Adoption of Arabic numerals
(C) Anatomical knowledge
(D) Steam-powered industry

43. Which two Muslim cities retain the greatest symbolic or religious significance in Islam to this day?

  I. Baghdad
  II. Istanbul
  III. Mecca
  IV. Timbuktu
  V. Medina

(A) I and II
(B) II and III
(C) II and IV
(D) III and V

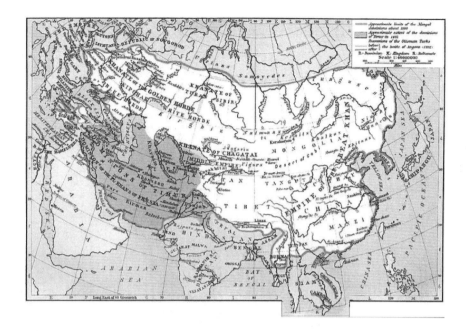

44. Which long-distance trade network was stabilized in the period historians term the Pax Mongolica (Mongol Peace)?

    (A) Indian Ocean routes
    (B) Triangular trade routes
    (C) East Asian sea routes
    (D) Silk Roads

45. Based on the map above, the Mongol empire stretched as far east as

    (A) Central Asia
    (B) Russia
    (C) Korea
    (D) Arabian Peninsula

—Ceramic piece, *Western Musicians on a Camel,* Tang dynasty

46. Which of the following conclusions can be made?
    (A) The diffusion of culture flowed from Japan to China and the rest of East Asia.
    (B) Sea links existed with the East African coast using steam boats.
    (C) The use of animal power was replaced by industrialization during the Song dynasty.
    (D) Economic and cultural links existed between East Asia and the Middle East.

47. The image above bests supports which of the following conclusions?
    (A) Transportation was suited to climate and topography.
    (B) Religious beliefs governed the treatment of animals.
    (C) There was a decrease in ceramic technology after the Han dynasty.
    (D) There was a lack of diffusion in music from China.

Special ambassadors [reported] that a monstrous . . . race of men had taken possession of the extensive, rich lands of the east . . . If [the Saracens] themselves could not withstand the attacks of such people, nothing remained to prevent their devastating the countries of the West. . . . [Regarding their] cruelty . . . there can be no infamy [great enough]. . . . The Tartar[s] . . . fed upon their [victim's] carcasses . . . and left nothing but the bones for the vultures.

Source: Matthew Paris, quoted in *Storm from the East*

Their style of conversation is courteous; they . . . have an air of good breeding, and eat their victuals with particular cleanliness. To their parents they show the utmost reverence. . . . The order . . . of all ranks of people, when they present themselves before his majesty ought not to pass unnoticed. When they approach . . . [him] they show their respect . . . by assuming a humble, placid, and quiet demeanor.

Source: Marco Polo, quoted in *Genghis Khan and Mongol Rule*

48. What impact would Matthew Paris's description have on Europeans?
    (A) They would have feared the Mongols as barbaric warriors.
    (B) They would have welcomed the Mongols as fellow warrior peoples.
    (C) They would have been confused based on the different names Paris used.
    (D) They would have been felt confident that Christ would protect them.

49. Which of the following is true of the above description of the Mongols by Marco Polo?
    (A) It is a secondary source on the Mongols
    (B) It complements Matthew Paris's account
    (C) It reinforces the view of the Mongols as barbaric
    (D) It contradicts Matthew Paris's negative account

—Mongol Passport made of iron with silver inlay. The script is Phagspa, a written language developed by Tibetan monks for the Mongolian empire. It reads:

By the strength of Eternal Heaven,
an edict of the Emperor [Khan].
He who has no respect shall be guilty.

50. The image above is best understood in the context of which of the following?
    (A) The spread of Islam to Central Asia
    (B) Eurasian metallurgy technology
    (C) The historical era, Pax Mongolia
    (D) The retraction of urbanization

51. The above Mongol passport represents which of the following?
    (A) State promotion of trade activity
    (B) Non-state promotion of trade activity
    (C) Merchants upset at their low status
    (D) Barriers against cultural connections

52. The use of Tibetan script by the Mongols is similar to which of the following?

    (A) The Mongol use of horses and Bactrian camels
    (B) The conversion to Islam among most Mongol rulers
    (C) The Mongol conquest of China and Russia
    (D) The Mongol practice of nonhereditary rulers

53. How were individuals selected for leadership in traditional Mongol society?

    (A) Hereditary warrior lineage
    (B) Long-established aristocratic status
    (C) Merit system based on demonstrated battlefield bravery
    (D) Divine revelation of chosen ones

54. Which of the following does not belong in a list of military tactics or equipment employed by the Mongol armies?

    (A) Combination of light and heavy cavalry
    (B) Use of the crossbow and short bow
    (C) Lightweight armor of leather, iron, or silk
    (D) Phalanx infantry formations

55. Which of the following terms for a political unit does not have the title of its leader as its root word?

    (A) Khanate
    (B) County
    (C) Nation
    (D) Shogunate

—Qutb Minar tower built to celebrate the victory of the Delhi Sultanate over the Hindu Kingdom near Delhi. The building in front with the white dome is the tomb of the saint Imam Zamin.

56. The image above represents which of the following changes in historical India in the later part of the Postclassical Era?

(A) Construction using stone as building materials

(B) The beginning of Islamic rule in Northern India

(C) The banning of entry to lower caste families

(D) The carving of Hindu inscriptions on monuments

57. The Qutb Minar seems to have been built to represent which of the following?

(A) The introduction of Islam into India by sea-going merchants and traders

(B) A tall brick observatory to study astronomy, astrology, and geography

(C) The triumph of Islam over Hinduism through monumental architecture

(D) The collapse of Sufi Islamic practices and dome architecture

—"Dance of Sufi Dervishes." Unknown author, from the illustrated book *Divane Hafez Shirazi*, circa 1480.

58. A historical argument on the popularity of Sufi practices in India is that it was due to

(A) The division of Islam into two sects, Sunni and Shia

(B) The influence of Indian culinary traditions

(C) Constant conflict among Indian Hindus

(D) A focus on spirituality and less on doctrines

59. Which of the following terms best describes Sufi Islam?
    (A) Fundamentalist
    (B) Mystical
    (C) Syncretic
    (D) Animist

60. Confucianism, Hinduism, and Christianity had what in common?
    (A) They directed attention to the afterlife.
    (B) They helped justify and preserve social inequality.
    (C) They urged the importance of political activity.
    (D) They stressed the value of warfare.

61. Which choice best describes the eastern and western geographic limits of Islamic rule at its greatest extent during the period of the Islamic caliphates in the Postclassical Era?
    (A) Northwest India to Spain and Morocco
    (B) Eastern Mediterranean to Persia
    (C) Arabian peninsula to the Tigris-Euphrates Valley
    (D) Persia to Southeast Asia

62. By the Postclassical Era, which beliefs do Hinduism and Buddhism still have in common?
    (A) Belief in the caste system
    (B) Damnation for sinners
    (C) Reverence for Muhammad
    (D) Reincarnation

Again as in the case of West Africa, trade brought culture as well as political changes to east Africa. Like their counterparts in West Africa, the ruling elites and wealthy merchants of East Africa converted to the Islamic faith. They did not necessarily give up their religious and cultural traditions but rather continued to observe them for purposes of providing cultural leadership for their societies. By adopting Islam, however, they laid a cultural foundation for close cooperation with Muslim merchants trading in the Indian Ocean. Moreover Islam served as a fresh source of legitimacy for their rule, since they gained recognition from Islamic states in Southwest Asia, and their conversion opened the door to political alliances with Muslim rulers in other lands. Even though the conversion of elite classes, did not bring about the immediate spread of Islam throughout their societies, it enabled Islam to establish a presence in East Africa

—Jeremy Bentley, in *Traditions and Encounters*

63. The above reading demonstrates which of the following

    (A) The conversion to Islam in West Africa was from the bottom up.
    (B) West African rulers and elite saw clear benefits in converting to Islam.
    (C) Trade played little role in spreading Islam to West Africa.
    (D) Islam entered East Africa from Southern European traders.

64. Based on the secondary source above, in West Africa, the practice of Islam

    (A) coexisted with previous forms of worship like animism
    (B) completely replaced animism and other belief systems
    (C) linked West Africa directly with South East Asia
    (D) established a caste system similar to that in India

The women there have "friends" and "companions" amongst the men out-side their own families, and the men in the same way have "companions" amongst the women of other families. A man may go into his house and find his wife entertaining her "companion" but he takes no objection to it. One day at Iwalatan I went into the qadi's (Islamic judge) house, after asking his permission to enter, and found with him a young woman of remarkable beauty. When I saw her I was shocked and turned to go out, but she laughed at me, instead of being overcome by shame, and the qadi said to me "Why are you going out? She is my companion." I was amazed at their conduct, for he was a theologian and a pilgrim [to Mecca] to boot. I was told that he had asked the sultan's permission to make the pilgrimage that year with his "companion"—whether this one or not I cannot say—but the sultan would not grant it.

Source: Ibn Battuta, a Muslim traveler to Mali,
1351–1353 recounts his experiences

65. Which of the following best describes Ibn Battuta's viewpoint toward his fellow Muslims in Mali?
    (A) Approving
    (B) Indifferent
    (C) Friendly
    (D) Critical

66. Based on the above text, what Ibn Battuta most disapproved of was

    (A) West African gender and marriage relations
    (B) The lack of Islamic judges or qadi
    (C) The Malians being less than friendly
    (D) The long journey required of pilgrimage

—"A West African king [Mansa Musa] holding a gold nugget" in a Spanish Catalan Atlas dated 1375.

67. Which of the following conclusions can be deducted from the map above?
    (A) The African gold trade was integral to Europe during the fourteenth century.
    (B) Europeans had no knowledge of camels as a method of transportation.
    (C) The West African Malian king, Mansa Musa was unknown to Europeans.
    (D) Europeans had no interest in West Africa trade or its people.

68. Based on your knowledge of the Trans-Saharan trade network of the Postclassical Africa, which item was purportedly traded for gold in equal weights?
    (A) Feathers
    (B) Fabrics
    (C) Salt
    (D) Copper

69. The Malian king, Mansa Musa is most famous in the West for which of the following acts?
    (A) banning the sale of Africans to Europeans or Arab slave traders
    (B) his lavish fourteenth-century pilgrimage to Mecca and Medina
    (C) converting to and helping to spread Roman Catholic Christianity
    (D) boosting the local economies of North Africa and Southern Europe

Source #1: One of eight bird monoliths, made of soapstone and found in the ruins of Great Zimbabwe.

Source #2: Ruins of Great Zimbabwe, circa 1200–1400.

70. The photo above of the ruins in southern Africa best demonstrates the existence of which of the following aspects of life in Southern Africa?

(A) Small colonies of Roman craftsmen who first settled in Southern Africa

(B) Nomadic groups who were skilled in the building of religious architecture

(C) A civilization with enough surpluses of food to support skilled crafts workers

(D) A strict caste society based on the worship of animal-themed deities

71. By 1500 which of the following changes occurred in Zimbabwe?
    (A) It began to dominate the export of slaves in the Indian Ocean.
    (B) It sent Christian missionaries north to Ethiopia and Sudan.
    (C) It became a world famous center of Islamic learning.
    (D) It declined due to various causes and was abandoned.

72. Which of the following was the common unifying feature of sub-Saharan African societies in the postclassical era?
    (A) Adoption of Islam by elites
    (B) Broad-based expansion of literacy among the masses of the people
    (C) Common Bantu linguistic roots
    (D) Atlantic Ocean trade-based economy

73. Which global force was the FIRST to consistently integrate sub-Saharan Africa into a global network of exchange of goods and ideas?
    (A) Islamic civilization
    (B) Modern globalization
    (C) Transatlantic slave trade
    (D) The Roman Empire

74. Which of the following materials is most associated with premodern sub-Saharan African artistic expertise?
    (A) Marble
    (B) Oil paints
    (C) Mosaic tile
    (D) Ivory

75. Which African society held on most fiercely to Christianity in the period of Islam's expansion in Africa?
    (A) Ethiopia
    (B) Mali
    (C) Ghana
    (D) Songhai

—Spanish colonial-era drawing of a native Incan with a *quipu*.

76. The image above of the quipu shows that the Incas
    (A) established contacts with ancient Egyptians
    (B) had a fully formed writing system
    (C) wore quipu to ritual human sacrifices
    (D) developed a method of keeping records

77. The Incas developed the quipu due to which historical fact?
    (A) They borrowed the quipu system from visiting Phoenician merchants.
    (B) Their complex and growing empire demanded a system of record keeping.
    (C) They brought the system with them when they migrated from Siberia.
    (D) It was also widely used in China and adapted to the Americas.

—Map of South America showing topographical information and the extent of the Incan empire.

78. Based on the map above, which of the following is true?

(A) The Incas overcame difficult geographic challenges.
(B) The Incas ruled over the Amazon Rainforest.
(C) The Incas were heavily influenced by the Maya.
(D) The Incas did not build cities or urban centers.

79. Which of the following best describes the region where the Inca civilization flourished?

(A) Amazon basin and rainforest
(B) Mexican plateau and highlands
(C) Andean highland and Pacific Coast
(D) Yucatan peninsula and pampas

—Photograph of Incan terrace farming and ruins.

80. The image above of Incan terrace farming is most similar to agricultural techniques in which of the following areas of the world?
    (A) Russia
    (B) China
    (C) India
    (D) England

81. Which of the following crops were grown in the Incan Empire?
    (A) Rice, corn, and cabbage
    (B) Wheat, barley, and oats
    (C) Sorghum, maize, and beats
    (D) Potatoes, corn, and beans

82. The farming techniques shown above are labor intensive. One continuity in the labor system used by both the Incas and the Spanish conquistadors is which of the following?
    (A) Slave labor
    (B) Nita labor
    (C) Indentured servitude
    (D) Wage labor

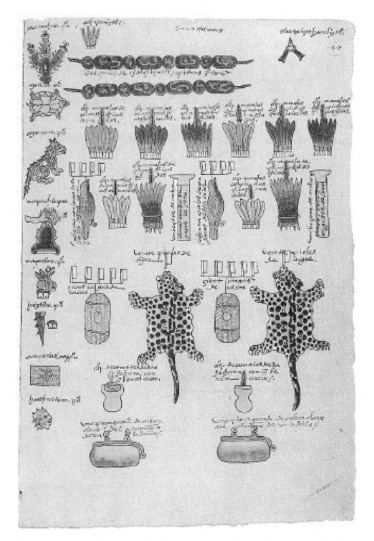

—Illustrated page from the Codex Mendoza. Created circa 1542 to show goods from neighboring cities that were delivered to Tenochtitlan, the Mexica capital. The goods include gems, feathers, jaguar pelts, and cacao.

83. Which of the following historical claims about the Aztec state can be supported based on the image?

(A) The Aztec kept records used a writing system borrowed from China.

(B) The Aztecs were military dominated by the growing Incan empire.

(C) The Aztecs were sent rare and valuable tributary goods by neighboring states.

(D) The Aztecs traded with the European states, such as France and England.

84. Which of the following is a limitation of the preceding image as an accurate source of information about the Aztec empire?

    (A) It was created by the Spanish after their conquest of the Aztecs.
    (B) It was written by the official Aztec scribes who later died.
    (C) It was biased since it was later stored in Christian monasteries.
    (D) It includes rare and valuable trade goods like bird feathers.

85. The historical situation in the image on the previous page will later contribute to which of the following events?

    (A) The Spanish will easily gain Indian allies in their conquest of the Aztecs.
    (B) The non-Aztecs will soon demand better trade conditions with the English.
    (C) The level of trade between the Aztecs and neighboring states will increase.
    (D) The trade between the Aztecs and its neighbors will become seaborne.

86. All of the following statements concerning Aztec human sacrifices are accurate EXCEPT:

    (A) It was a preexisting religious ritual as the Aztecs rose to power.
    (B) It was accompanied at times by ritual cannibalism of the victims.
    (C) It was pointed to by conquistadores to justify Spanish colonization.
    (D) Members of the Aztec ruling elite were the sacrificial victims.

87. Aztec and Incan civilizations managed to construct monumental structures without which of the following?

    (A) Writing systems
    (B) State authority
    (C) Draft animals
    (D) Stone tools

88. Which of the following best characterizes similarities between Aztec and Inca civilizations?
    I. Grew out of preceding civilizations
    II. Nobility formed the personal of the state
    III. Climatic and topographical setting
    (A) I and II
    (B) II and III
    (C) II only
    (D) III only

89. Which of the following best explains the geographic spread of Inuit people from Alaska to Greenland?
    (A) Their knowledge of Indian Ocean winds to travel long distances
    (B) Their galleons and use of the astrolabe to navigate by
    (C) Their continuing ability to adapt to harsh environments
    (D) Their syncretic belief systems based on the geographic features

90. In comparison to the indigenous Inuit societies, the Greenland Vikings
    (A) Thrived on walrus meat for food and ivory for trade
    (B) Slowly declined due to lack of food and disease
    (C) Built up large settlements and expanded to Iceland
    (D) Enthusiastically adapted to Inuit lifestyles and culture

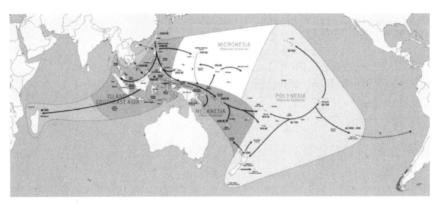

—Map showing the diaspora of Austronesian peoples across the Indo-Pacific oceans.

91. Which of the following Austronesian migrations is an unproven theory?

(A) The journey to Madagascar off the East coast of Africa

(B) The discovery and settlement of New Zealand

(C) Voyages taken across the Pacific to the Americas

(D) The colonization of the Hawaiian islands

92. The spread of the Austronesian language group is comparable to which of the following language groups?

(A) Bantu-speaking people throughout Africa

(B) Latin languages in Eastern Europe

(C) Arabic languages into South Asia

(D) Siberian languages to China

93. One explanation for the extent of the Austronesian/Polynesian spread across the Indo-Pacific oceans is due to which of the following?

(A) Their search for gold and silver sources

(B) The use of the compass and navigational charts

(C) Outrigger canoes and knowledge of trade winds

(D) Land bridges and small bodies of water

Source: Two medieval illustrations (*August, June*) in the Book of Hours by Pol de Lumbourg, circa 1412–1416.

94. The image on the right of European society in the late Middle Ages is best understood in the context of which of the following truisms?

    (A) The power of the Roman Catholic Church over daily life.
    (B) The agricultural basis for the medieval economy
    (C) The possibility of social mobility that existed
    (D) The use of vernacular languages like English and French

95. One continuity that is exemplified by the two images is one of

    (A) Trade as the basis for the European economy
    (B) The use of Latin as the vernacular language
    (C) The lack of seasonal change in Europe
    (D) Widespread social inequality

I, John of Toul, make it known that I am the faithful man of the lady, Beatrice, Countess of Troyes, and my most dear lord, Theobald, Count of Champagne, her son against a person living or dead, except for my allegiance to lord, Enjorand of Coucy, Lord John of Arcis and the count of Grandpre. If it should happen that the count of Grandpre should be at war with the countess and the count of Champagne on his own quarrel, I will aid the count of Grandpre in my own person and will send to the count and countess of Champagne the knights whose service I own them for the fief which I hold of them.

—A Vassal Pledges Loyalty, circa 1200s

96. The text above concerning counts, vassals, and allegiances is in the context of which system of the European Middle Ages?

(A) Mercantilism
(B) Feudalism
(C) Chivalry
(D) Chinampas

97. In the Medieval Europe system above, in return for loyalty and military service, nobles would receive fiefs from their overlords, including land, houses, castles, and serf peasants. This system came about primarily due to a lack of which of the following conditions?

(A) Religious unity
(B) End of Viking attacks
(C) A centralized government
(D) A common language

98. In comparison, a similar system of land for loyalty among lords and their vassals developed in which of the following non-European countries?

(A) India
(B) Japan
(C) China
(D) Persia (Iran)

Hanseatic League Imports and Exports (March 18, 1368–March 10, 1369)

*In thousands of Port Lubeck marks

Imports		Origin, Destination	Exports		Total	%
150		London/Hamburg	38		188	34.4
44		Livonian towns	51		95	17.4
	10	Riga		14		
	34	Reval (Tallinn)		14.3		
	–	Pernau		22.7		
49.4		Scania	32.6		82	15
52		Gotland, Sweden	29.4		81.4	14.9
19		Prussian towns	29.5		48.5	8.9
	16	Danzig		22.8		
	3	Elbing		6.6		
17.2a		Wendish & Pomeranian towns	25.2		42.4	7.8
	5.5	Stettin		7		
	4	Stralsund		7.5		
	2.2	Rostock		4.6		
	5.5	Wismar		6.1		
4.3		Begen	–		4.3	0.8
3		Small Baltic ports	1.2		4.2	0.8
338.9		Total	206.9		545.8	100

99. Based on the table above, which of the following is true of Hanseatic League trade in the 1200–1450 period?

    (A) Trade grew stagnant in this time period
    (B) Exports exceed imports in every port
    (C) Imports were more than exports
    (D) London was outside its scope

100. The Hanseatic League trade greatly contributed to which of the following historical processes?

    (A) The Italian Renaissance
    (B) The European Crusades
    (C) The Age of Absolutism
    (D) The Northern Renaissance

The King to the Sheriff of Kent, Greeting: Because a great part of the people and especially of workmen and servants, having died in the plague, many seeing the great necessity of masters and scarcity of servants, will not serve unless they may receive excessive wages . . . we . . . upon deliberation and in consul with nobles and learned men assisting us, declare that every man and woman of our realm of England of what condition he be, free or bound, able in body and within sixty years of age, having no craft or land to occupy himself and not serving any other . . . he shall be bound to serve him who shall require him and take only the wages or salary which were accustomed in England five or six years before.

If any workman or servant retained in any man's service, do depart from the said service without reasonable cause or license, he shall have pain of imprisonment and no one, upon the same penalty, shall receive such a person in his service.

No one, moreover, shall pay or promise to pay to any one more wages or salary than was accustomed as is said before.

—King Edward III of England's Statute on Laborers, 1351

101. Which of the following changes are behind the statute above?
    (A) The switch of a system to wage labor from coerced labor
    (B) The introduction of New World crops like wheat and potatoes
    (C) The end of labor contract disputes between employers and employees
    (D) The influx of Asian spices and silk, which disrupted the economy

102. Which of the following historical developments caused the change in working relationships as shown in the King Edward III of England's Statute on Laborers?
    (A) The European Crusades
    (B) The Hanseatic League
    (C) The Reformation
    (D) The Bubonic Plague

103. What was the main global impact of the Crusades?
    I. Western Europeans gained permanent bases in the Middle East.
    II. Islam split into the Sunni and Shia branches.
    III. Western Europeans were reintroduced to the knowledge and trade of a more civilized world.
    IV. Christianity became the dominant religion in Jerusalem.
    (A) I, II, and III
    (B) I, II, and IV
    (C) III and IV
    (D) III only

104. Which of the following do historians most closely associate with the period of Western history known as the High Middle Ages?

(A) Carolingian France

(B) Steam-powered Industrial Revolution

(C) Enclosure movement and the rise of commercial agriculture

(D) Gothic architecture, the Crusades, and the rise of the Western University

105. Which group was most likely to be literate in the period of European history often called the Dark Ages?

(A) Aristocrats

(B) Peasants

(C) Monks

(D) Knights

106. Which of the following terms matches this definition: "agricultural laborer tied to a piece of land with rights to military protection, heritable ownership of a plot of land, and owing obligations to share crop yields each season with his or her lord."

(A) peasants

(B) slaves

(C) apprentices

(D) serfs

—The mosaic of Emperor Justinian and his retinue.

107. The above image shows the Byzantine emperor flanked by military and ecclesiastical figures. This plus the halo around his head shows that Justinian and his successors till 1453 justified his rule through the principle of

(A) Hagia Sophia
(B) Pater familias
(C) Senatorial privilege
(D) Caesaropapism

108. Which of the following European regions felt the influence of Byzantine civilization in the postclassical era?

(A) Russia
(B) Iberian peninsula
(C) Scandinavia
(D) British isles

The circumference of the city of Constantinople is eighteen miles; half of it is surrounded by the sea, and half by land, and it is situated upon two arms of the sea, one turning from the sea of Russia [the Black Sea], and one from the sea of Sepharad [the Mediterranean].

All sorts of merchants come here from the land of Babylon, from the land of Shinar [Mesopotamia], from Persia, Media [western Iran], and all the sovereignty of the land of Egypt, from the land of Canaan [Palestine], and the empire of Russia, from Hungary, Patzinakia [Ukraine], Khazaria [southern Russia], and the land of Lombardy [northern Italy] and Sepharad [Spain].

Constantinople is a busy city, and merchants come to it from every country by sea or land, and there is none like it in the world except Baghdad, the great city of Islam. In Constantinople is the church of Hagia Sophia, and the seat of the pope of the Greeks, since Greeks do not obey the pope of Rome. There are also as many churches as there are days of the year. . . . And in this church [Hagia Sophia] there are pillars of gold and silver, and lamps of silver and gold more than a man can count.

From every part of the Byzantine empire tribute is brought here every year, and they fill strongholds with garments of silk, purple, and gold. Like unto these storehouses and this wealth there is nothing in the whole

world to be found. It is said that the tribute of the city amounts every year to 20,000 gold pieces, derived both from the rents of shops and markets and from the tribute of merchants who enter by sea or land.

—The Itinerary of Rabbi Benjamin Tudela, 12th century. Medieval Jewish traveler.

109. According to Rabbi Tudela in the above reading, which of the following was true of the city of Constantinople?
    (A) It was at the crossroads of trade and cultural exchange.
    (B) It was impressive but still not an equal to London.
    (C) It was a counterpoint to the city of Rome.
    (D) It was dominated by the Persian minority.

110. Which historical event is Rabbi Benjamin Tudela referring to when he writes that the Greeks "do not obey the pope of Rome"?
    (A) The Protestant Reformation
    (B) The Great Schism
    (C) The Magyar invasions
    (D) The Feudal order

—Mongol attack on Suzdal, Russia in 1238.

111. Which of the following best describes Russia's status after the historical event in the image above?

(A) Colonial possession

(B) Trade network

(C) Fiefdom

(D) Tributary state

112. Which of the following historical arguments can be made about the impact of Mongol control over Russia?
    (A) Russia was held back by being cut off from Western Europe.
    (B) Russia was integrated into the long distance Chinese trade.
    (C) Russia has never been defeated due to its weather and size.
    (D) Serfdom in Russia was established on orders from the Mongols.

113. After the fall of the western portion of the Roman Empire, the official tongue in Constantinople shifted from Latin to which of the following?
    (A) Turkish
    (B) Persian
    (C) Chinese
    (D) Greek

114. The Byzantine Empire flourished as a crossroads of trade from which regions?
    (A) Mediterranean, the Middle East, and Asia
    (B) India, Mediterranean, and Asia
    (C) Sub-Saharan Africa, India, and the Middle East
    (D) The Middle East, Asia, and Scandinavia

115. Russian civilization emerged nearest to what modern-day city?
    (A) St. Petersburg
    (B) Kiev
    (C) Moscow
    (D) Warsaw

116. Which of the following does NOT belong in a list of similarities between Byzantine and dynastic Chinese political rule in the Song era?
    (A) An imperial bureaucracy staffed by persons from all social classes but generally drawn from the aristocracy
    (B) A royal throne held always by a powerful women
    (C) An emperor whose rule has God's approval
    (D) Territorial loss to semi-nomadic warriors

—The Lewis chessmen were made from walrus ivory from the Arctic circle, carved in Trondheim, Norway, and later found in the Hebrides islands north of Scotland but thought to have been on their way to the Viking port city of Dublin in Ireland.

Photo by Sean McManamon

117. Which of the following provides some context for the Lewis chessmen and the board game of chess in general?
    (A) Economic links between the Aztecs of Mesoamerica and the Viking world of Northern Europe
    (B) A wider cultural connection with India via the Middle East since chess originated in India
    (C) A religious connection with the non-violent tenants of Chinese Buddhism
    (D) The syncretic nature of Scandinavian Christianity and Shamanic Siberian peoples

118. The method of movement of the Lewis chessmen shows a similarity to the which of the following trade networks?

(A) Silk Road
(B) Arabian peninsula
(C) Tran Saharan
(D) Indian Ocean

119. Which of the following is true of the ivory Lewis Chessmen as a trade item?

(A) It was a staple food and a manufactured good.
(B) It was a luxury item but also a raw material.
(C) It was a manufactured good and a luxury item.
(D) It was a raw material but banned at the time.

120. The Romanesque artistic style of the Lewis chessmen and other art from the mid-twelfth to the fourteenth centuries has been labeled as a pre-renaissance by scholars. Which of the following is true about this historical argument?

(A) It supports the idea that artistic renewals comes from economic depressions.
(B) It refutes the idea of the later Italian Renaissance as a break with the post-classical.
(C) It is put forth primarily by Eurocentric scholars who value non-European over European achievements.
(D) It clashes with the Gothic style of art from the Islamic world.

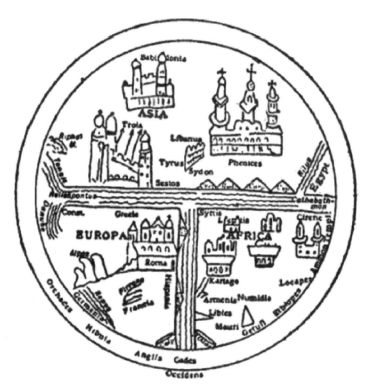

—T and O maps are a figurative and conceptual type of medieval cartography that represents only the top-half of a spherical Earth, circa 1200.

121. The medieval T-O map with Jerusalem in the center is best understood in the context of
    (A) The Latin language
    (B) A Christian worldview
    (C) Judaic teachings
    (D) Trade winds

122. One change that can be inferred from the map above that took place in the following century was which of the following developments?
    (A) European knowledge of the world slowly increased.
    (B) Europeans discovered that Africa was smaller than thought.
    (C) Europeans saw the city of Rome as a more accurate center of the world.
    (D) Europeans relied more on East Asian conceptions of the world.

123. Which of the following is true based on the evidence shown in the T-O map?

    (A) It did not show a division between Asia and Europe.
    (B) It displays the world as a round sphere.
    (C) It is incomplete in its number of continents shown.
    (D) It does not include bodies of water.

124. Throughout the world, by 1400 which of the following technologies will help eliminate castles as secure fortifications?

    (A) Sailing instruments like the compass
    (B) Stirrups and saddles for horses
    (C) Catapults and crossbows
    (D) Gunpowder weapons like cannons

CHAPTER 2

The Early Modern Era: 1450 to 1750

Controlling Idea: The First Global Age

In this unit the big news, so to speak, is that the Americas are integrated into global long distance trade networks for the first time. While all civilizations are in ever closer contact, it is the West that works its way to the center of the world trading network, serving as intermediaries in the ever greater volumes of trade that wash across the globe between 1450 and 1750. This integration also sees waves of migration across the world with settlers spreading out from the Old World to the New World. This includes unwilling migrants of Africans being forcibly transported to the Americas as slaves for the benefit of the West. While not dominant by 1750 (except over the Americas), the West nonetheless is becoming positioned to capitalize off its emergent role at the "core" of a new world economy, and the slow integration of the world into a single economic unit begins in this period and has accelerated down to today.

This image was donated to Wiki commons by the Metropolitan Museum of Art in NYC

I want to go further,
But my legs are bruised and scratched.
The bony rocks appear chiseled,
The pines look as if they had been dyed.
Sitting down, I feel like a small bird,
As I look out at the crowd of peaks gathered before me.
Having ascended the heights to the brink of the abyss,
I hold fast and ponder the need to sincerely face criticism.
Wherever a road ends, I will set myself down,
Wherever a source opens, I will build a temple.
All this suffices to nourish my eyes,
And rest my feet.

—*Wooded Mountains at Dusk*, by Kuncan, 1666.

125. The preceding Chinese poem and painting best shows the influence of which belief system?
    (A) Daoism
    (B) Islam
    (C) Confucianism
    (D) Christianity

126. Which of the following was true of the three Chinese arts shown on the preceding page: painting, poetry, and calligraphy?
    (A) These arts were dismissed by the emperor's court as frivolous.
    (B) These arts were officially banned for merchants.
    (C) These arts were not tested by the civil service exams.
    (D) These arts were largely the domain of the scholar gentry class.

When the Portgualls come to . . . China, to traffic they must remain there but certain days. And when they come in at the gate of the city they must enter their names in a book and when they go out at night they put out their names. They must not lie in the town all night but lie in their boats without the town. The Chinese are very suspicious and does not trust strangers

—Ralph Fitch's Journal in the late sixteenth century describing the Portuguese arrival in China.

127. Based on the reading above, which of the following represents a change in East Asia in the Early Modern Era (1450–1750)?

(A) The Mongols conquered Japan in a series of naval invasions.
(B) Europeans arrived in Asia in search of direct trade.
(C) Merchants were looked down upon in Chinese society.
(D) Trade winds helped Europeans sail across the Indian Ocean.

128. Based on the reading above, which of the following represents a continuity in East Asia?

(A) China maintained a strong xenophobic attitude toward outsiders.
(B) China built boats that had multiple sleeping berths in them.
(C) The Portuguese spread Buddhism to China from Europe.
(D) The Chinese were open to outsiders and foreign traders.

Our Confucian teaching is based on the Five Relationships (between parent and child, ruler and minister, husband and wife, older and younger brothers, and friends), whilst the Lord of Heaven Jesus was crucified because he plotted against his own country, showing that he did not recognize the relationship between ruler and subject. Mary, the mother of Jesus, had a husband named Joseph, but she said Jesus was not conceived by him.

Those who follow this teaching [Christianity] are not allowed to worship their ancestors and ancestral tablets. They do not recognize the relationship of parent and child. Their teachers oppose the Buddhists and Daoists, who do recognize the relationship between ruler and subject and father and son. Jesus did not recognize the relationship between ruler and subject and parent and child, and yet the Christians speak of him as recognizing these relationships. What [arrogant] nonsense! . . .

—Yang Guangxian between 1659 and 1665

129. The attitudes above are best understood in the context of which of the following?

   (A) Pro-Buddhist and Daoist sentiments
   (B) Anti-Christian and xenophobic attitudes
   (C) Chinese tribute and trade systems
   (D) Chinese abandonment of Confucianism

130. Which of the following was a long-term result of the introduction of Christianity into China in the sixteenth century?

   (A) Christianity became the new official state religion of the Qing dynasty in 1644.
   (B) Christianity did not become popular with the vast majority of Chinese people.
   (C) Christianity was spread by Central Asian nomads along the Silk Road.
   (D) Christianity was adopted by the merchants but rejected by the warrior caste.

—Frontispiece for Athanasius Kircher's *China Illustrated*, published at Amsterdam, 1667. The figures depicted are Jesuits such as missionaries, Adam Schall and Matteo Ricci holding a map of China and St. Francis Xavier and Ignatius Loyola venerating an IHS representing Jesus Christ surrounded by angels.

131. The push to spread Roman Catholic Christianity by the Jesuits needs to be understood in the European context of which of the following?
    (A) The Spanish Inquisition
    (B) The Peasants' Rebellion
    (C) The Anglican Compromise
    (D) The Counter-Reformation

132. The depiction of the missionary Adam Schall in Chinese dress was evidence of which of the following practices of the Jesuits in China?
    (A) The plan to disguise their identity from the Chinese authorities
    (B) The attempt to dress as native scholars so as to appear less foreign
    (C) The difficulty in obtaining European clerical clothing in Asia
    (D) The trade in silk along a network of roads from Asia to Europe

1. *Strengthen filial piety and brotherly affection to emphasize human relations.*
2. *Strengthen clan relations to illustrate harmony.*
3. *Pacify relations between local groups to put an end to quarrels and litigation.*
4. *Stress agriculture and sericulture so that there may be sufficient food and clothing.*
5. *Prize frugality so as to make careful use of wealth.*
6. *Promote education to improve the habits of scholars.*
7. *Extirpate heresy to exalt orthodoxy.*
8. *Speak of the law to give warning to the stupid and stubborn.*
9. *Clarify rites and manners to improve customs.*
10. *Let each work at his own occupation so that the people's minds will be settled.*
11. *Instruct young people to prevent them from doing wrong.*
12. *Prevent false accusations to shield the law-abiding.*
13. *Prohibit sheltering of runaways to avoid being implicated in their crime.*
14. *Pay taxes to avoid being pressed for payment.*
15. *Unite the baojia system to eliminate theft and armed robbery.*
16. *Resolve hatred and quarrels to respect life.*

—The Sacred Edict of the Kangxi Emperor, 1670.

133. The promotion of "filial piety" and "brotherly affection" in the first edict, are clear references to which philosophy in traditional China?

(A) Buddhism
(B) Daoism
(C) Legalism
(D) Confucianism

134. Which of the following was a historical argument on the motivations behind Kangxi's Sacred Edict?

(A) The Qing dynasty were non-Han Chinese and had to appear to be following traditional Chinese governing precepts to avoid revolts.
(B) The Qing dynasty had overthrown the Mongol Yuan dynasty and wanted to restore Mongol rule and traditional practices.
(C) Having won the Opium War over the French, the Qing sought to reestablish their control over the waterways along the Eastern coast.
(D) The Qing State was decentralizing their power and left much of the country to govern themselves under traditional precepts.

135. How do historians explain the Ming dynasty's 1433 decision to abandon the treasure ship voyages to the Indian Ocean basin that could have placed China at the core of the developing world economy?

(A) State resources were required to thwart nomadic incursions from beyond the Great Wall.

(B) A dominant neo-Confucian worldview de-emphasized the value of non-Chinese ideas and products.

(C) State-backed exploration of distant lands was an unusual experiment in Chinese history.

(D) All of the above.

136. Aside from the Yuan, which other Chinese dynasty was founded by nomadic invaders?

(A) Qing (Manchu)

(B) Ming

(C) Song

(D) Han

137. By 1750, what was the most populous region on the globe?

(A) Sub-Saharan Africa

(B) Western Europe

(C) East Asia

(D) South America

138. Which European trade product met with the greatest demand in East Asia in the period?

(A) Opium

(B) Bullion (precious metals)

(C) Silk

(D) Mechanical clocks

—Woodblock print showing Samurai Selling Armor to a Scrap Metal Merchant. 1797.

139. Which of the following acts as context for the situation in the image on the woodblock print?

(A) The Tokugawa shogunate drafted merchants into their military.

(B) The Tokugawa era was one of cultural homogeneity.

(C) The Pax Tokugawa made most of the samurai warriors obsolete.

(D) The Tokugawa era was largely one of economic depression.

140. In comparison to Japan, in Europe which of the following is true concerning the warrior classes?

(A) Many took religious vows and left politics.

(B) They adapted to gunpowder weapons.

(C) They were defeated during the Crusades.

(D) They stopped using horses by 1500 ce.

141. In Tokugawa Japan, merchants ranked lower than samurai according to Confucian principles. Which of the following reflects a conflicting idea behind the image above?

(A) The metal in the swords was worth less money than their clothes.

(B) Samurai swords were no longer valued compared to guns.

(C) Merchants and trade were banished to Japan's outlying islands.

(D) Many samurai were economically struggling compared to the merchants.

1. Japanese ships are strictly forbidden to leave for foreign countries.

2. No Japanese is permitted to go abroad. If there is anyone who attempts to do so secretly, he must be executed. The ship so involved must be impounded and its owner arrested and the matter must be reported to the higher authority.

3. If any Japanese returns from overseas after residing there, he must be put to death.

4. If there is any place where the teachings of padres (Christianity) is practiced, the two of you must order a thorough investigation . . .

7. If there are any Southern Barbarians (Westerners) who propagate the teachings of padres, or otherwise commit crimes, they may be incarcerated in the prison maintained by the Omura domain, as previously . . .

10. Samurai are not permitted to purchase any goods originating from foreign ships directly from Chinese merchants in Nagasaki.

—The Edicts of the Tokugawa Shogunate in Japan, 1615

142. The shogun's policies regarding foreign trade as described in the excerpt had which purpose?
(A) To limit foreign ideas and prevent threats to the shogun's power
(B) To become dominant in East Asian trading networks
(C) To stop Japanese merchants from evading taxation on trade goods
(D) To prevent individual ports from monopolizing trade

143. Which of the following was an effect of the Japanese seclusion policies described in the excerpts?
(A) The Tokugawa Shogunate faced rebellions as a result of economic decline.
(B) Japan had limited knowledge of foreign technology and culture.
(C) The Tokugawa Shogunate was overthrown by Japanese merchants.
(D) Japan was completely isolated from regional trade networks.

144. Which of the following changes in Japan policy concerning interactions occurred under the Tokugawa Shogunate?
(A) Japan increased its overseas trade in raw materials with Ming China and Korea.
(B) Japan saw a decrease in the populace's practice of Chinese Daoism and Shamanism.
(C) Japan adopted a policy of almost total isolation with the exception of limited trade at Nagasaki.
(D) Japan promoted the use of diplomacy with China and European nations rather than warfare.

1. *Live an honest and sincere life. Respect your parents, your brothers, and your relatives, and try to live harmoniously with them all. Honor and treat with respect everyone you meet, even those you see only occasionally. Never behave discourteously or selfishly. . . .*

2. *. . . Not one person in ten understands the things of this life nor of the next . . . If even Buddha himself is said to have known nothing, nothing of the world to come, how can any ordinary mortal know such things? Until you reach fifty, therefore, do not worry about the future life . . .*

4. *Until you are forty, avoid every luxury, and never act or think like one above your station in life. In matters of business and money making, however, work harder than anyone else . . . Until you turn fifty, be temperate in all things, and avoid all ostentation and finery, anything, in fact, that might call attention to yourself. Do not cultivate expensive tastes, for you should ignore such things as the tea ceremony, swords, daggers, and fine clothes.*

13. *Those with even a small fortune must remember that their duty in life is to devote themselves to their house and its business. They must not become careless, for if they buy what they want, do as they please, and, in general, live sumptuously, they will soon spend that fortune . . . Although a samurai can draw on the produce of his tenured lands to earn his livelihood, a merchant must rely on the profit from his business, for without that profit, the money in his bags would soon disappear. No matter how much profit he makes and packs into his bags, however, if he continually wastes that money, he may as well pack it into bags full of holes. Remember this. . . . These seventeen articles were written not for Sōshitsu's sake but for yours. They are his testament, and you should follow them closely. They should be as important to you as the Great Constitution of Prince Shōtoku. Read them every day, or even twice a day, and be careful to forget nothing.*

—Codes of Merchant Houses:
Excerpts from The Testament of Shimai Sōshitsu.

145. Which of the following was a direct cause of the historical situation described above?

(A) A period of peace and stability
(B) A time of war and conflict
(C) The arrival of the European traders
(D) The importation of Buddhism into Japan

146. Which of the following was a similar type of era in world history?

    (A) Mongol Empire invasions

    (B) Northern European renaissance

    (C) Conquest of the Americas

    (D) Islamic expansion

147. Which significance did Nagasaki Bay hold in Japanese history before the United States dropped a second atomic bomb there?

    (A) It was the imperial city of the Tokugawa regime and the home of the Japanese emperor

    (B) Invading Mongol navy was wrecked by a typhoon in a failed invasion attempt there

    (C) Mathew Perry's gunboat visit to Japan occurred there and Japan negotiated a treaty

    (D) Western trade was restricted to contact with the Dutch merchants at Dejima island

148. Which regional civilizations were able to pursue a policy of isolation in relation to the maritive West in the period 1450–1750?

    (A) West African

    (B) South Asia

    (C) Meso-American

    (D) East Asia

149. Which European power continued to trade in Japan in the period from the early 1600s to 1854?

    (A) Dutch

    (B) English

    (C) China

    (D) Portuguese

150. In comparison to the Chinese restrictions on the Portuguese, the Japanese differed in that they

    (A) Initially banned the Europeans from Tokyo but later opened up the nation in the 17th century to all traders and merchants

    (B) Travelled themselves to the New World in search of gold from South America mines

    (C) Attacked any Chinese or Koreans sailors who attempted to trade silk and porcelain at Nagasaki

    (D) At first valued the Portuguese as sources of gunpowder weapons but later imposed strict controls

What Heaven imparts to man is called human nature,

To follow our nature is called the Way.

It is rooted in the Mind and lodged in the Teachings

The forms through which it has been bequeathed to us are full of dignity

Eternal and age less as Heaven

—Excerpts from 16th century Vietnamese poet,
Nguyễn Bỉnh Khiêm's Inscription for "Three Belief" Temple

151. Which of the following Asian belief systems show a clear influence on the Vietnamese reading above?

(A) Confucianism
(B) Daoism
(C) Hinduism
(D) Christianity

152. Which of the following groups in Early Modern Vietnam would have been educated in the above belief systems?

(A) Peasants
(B) Merchants
(C) Scholars
(D) Aamurai

Long before Europeans arrived, maritime Southeast Asia (including present-day Malaysia, Indonesia and the Philippines) carried on a substantial long-distance trade. Many of the merchants were women—in some cases because commerce was thought too base an occupation for upper-class men, but too lucrative for elite families to abstain from completely. . .

the Portuguese, the first Europeans to establish themselves in this world, had found intermarrying with such women to be an indispensable part of creating profitable and defensible colonies. When the VOC gave up on importing Dutch women—having sometimes found "willing" candidates only in the orphanages or even brothels of Holland, and facing discontent among the intended husbands of these women—it turned to the daughters of these earlier Portuguese-Asian unions: they at least spoke a Western language and were at least nominally Christian. Many had also learned from their mothers how useful a European husband could be for protecting their business interests in an increasingly multinational and often violent trading world. . .

The VOC's principal goal, of course, was profit, and profit was best secured by monopolizing the export of all sorts of Asian goods—from pepper to porcelain—back to Europe. In theory, the company also claimed—at least intermittently—the right to license and tax (or sink) all the ships participating in the much larger intra-Asian trade, including those of Southeast Asia's women traders. But the realities of huge oceans and numerous rivals made enforcing such a system impossible, and the VOC also faced powerful enemies within. Most company servants soon discovered that while smuggling goods back to Holland was risky and difficult, they could earn sums by trading illegally (or semi-legally) within Asia that dwarfed their official salaries. Here their wives were a perfect vehicle for making a fortune: they were well connected in and knowledgeable about local markets, often possessed considerable capital and able to manage the family business continuously without being susceptible to sudden transfer by the company.

Source: Kenneth Pomeranz and Steven Topik, historians, *The World That Trade Created: Society, Culture and World Economy 1400 to the Present*, 2006.

153. Which of the following enabled the Dutch to establish and enforce a monopoly on the Southeast Asian spice trade in the seventeenth century?

(A) The establishment of powerful joint-stock companies
(B) The development of exclusive inventions for navigation
(C) Increased scientific knowledge leading to medicines to treat malaria
(D) Population growth as a result of the Columbian Exchange

154. Which of the following acts as context for the relationship between male European merchants and local Southeast Asian women merchants?

(A) Southeast Asia was primarily influenced by Chinese culture and beliefs.
(B) Southeast Asia was ruled by an all-powerful monarch in Northern India.
(C) Southeast Asia was not affected by seasonal monsoon or trade winds.
(D) Southeast Asia was not a strict patriarchy and women had some autonomy.

Sweet potato, found in Luzon,*
Grows all over, trouble-free
Foreign devils love to eat it
Propagates so easily.

We just made a single cutting
Boxed it up and brought it home
Ten years later, Fujian's saviour.
If it dies, just make a clone.

Take your cutting, then re-plant it
Wait a week and see it grow
This is how we cultivate it
In our homeland, reap and sow.

*location in the Philippines

—Excerpt from He Qiaoyuan's "Ode to the Sweet Potato", circa 1594

155. The poem above is clear evidence of which of the following?
   (A) China's military conquest of the Philippine islands including Luzon
   (B) Extensive trade contacts between China and outlying regions in Asia
   (C) Chinese borrowing of all European trade items and belief systems
   (D) Japan's use of terrace farming and rice agriculture from China

156. Which of the following was a direct result of the movement of the sweet potato and other New World food items into China?
   (A) Population migration
   (B) Population increase
   (C) Population decrease
   (D) Population stagnation

157. Which European power won the colony of Indonesia away from the Portuguese in the seventeenth century?
   (A) England
   (B) Spain
   (C) France
   (D) Holland

158. Which colony was claimed by Spain as a result of Ferdinand Magellan's circumnavigation of the globe in 1519-1521?
   (A) Madagascar
   (B) Philippines
   (C) Mexico
   (D) Hispaniola

Source: Photos from the Hagia Sophia in Istanbul, Turkey, showing minarets and large decorative shields with calligraphy inscriptions from the Koran. Photos by Sean McManamon.

159. The addition of Islamic minarets and the shields to the Hagia Sophia church after the Ottoman conquest of the Byzantine Empire and its capital city Constantinople is a result of all of the following EXCEPT:
    (A) Appropriation by a triumphalist Islam over Christianity
    (B) Conquest of Constantinople by the Ottoman Turks
    (C) Cultural blending of Islamic and Christian design
    (D) The welcoming of Muslims to the Byzantine church

160. The Hagia Sophia is now a national museum in Turkey's capital of Istanbul. This is best understood in the context of which of the following?
    (A) Mustapha Kemal Ataturk's secularization program
    (B) The military domination of government in postwar Turkey
    (C) The adoption of atheistic communism by Turkey
    (D) The success of Turkey in World War battlefields

Empire	Land Area	Approximate Population	Religion Composition	Estimated Size of Military	Source of Canons & Firearms
Ottoman Empire c. 1566	c. 1,200,000 square miles	20–35 million	Large majority Sunni; a significant Christian and small Jewish minorities	Largest army Recorded: 200,000 cavalry, infantry, artillery +90 warships	Produced locally
Safavid Empire c. 1600	c. 750,000 square miles	10–15 million	Majority Shi'a Muslims; small Sunni, Jewish, and Christian minorities	40,000-50,000 cavalry, infantry, artillery; no navy	Imported cannon not widely used, except by European mercenaries
Mughal Empire c. 1600	c. 1 million square miles	105–110 million	Ruling Muslim minority with great Hindu majority plus Sikh, Buddhist, Jain, and Christian minorities	200,000+ cavalry, infantry, artillery; no navy	Imported and produced locally

161. Which of the following conclusions is best supported by the data in the chart above?

(A) The spread of gunpowder weaponry helped these states dominate and retain power.

(B) The importation of gunpowder weaponry limited the reach of these states to Asia.

(C) Gunpowder eliminated forever the use of cavalry on Eurasian battlefields.

(D) The spread of gunpowder weaponry was initiated by Christian and Jewish minorities.

162. Based on a study of the chart on the previous page a historian of Muslim rule in the Early Modern World (1450–1750) would most likely support which of the following historical arguments?
    (A) The military might of Jewish minorities in the Middle East was a challenge for the Ottomans.
    (B) The Safavid empire easily dominated its Muslim neighbors, the Ottomans and Mughals.
    (C) Mughal rulers had a more difficult task of ruling over a large non-Muslim population.
    (D) With no Mughal navy, Mughals traders did little business with the outside world.

163. All of the following best explains the existence of a large Hindu majority in South Asia by the Mughal era EXCEPT:
    (A) Islam's relatively late arrival in a South Asia.
    (B) Hinduism's long establishment and state support
    (C) Islam offered social equality among its followers.
    (D) Hinduism absorbed many Buddhist and Jain beliefs.

No distinction is attached to birth among the Turks; the deference to be paid to a man is measured by the position he holds in the public service. There is no fighting for precedence; a man's place is marked out by the duties he discharges. In making his appointments the Sultan pays no regard to any pretensions on the score of wealth or rank, nor does he take into consideration recommendations or popularity, he considers each case on its own merits, and examines carefully into the character, ability, and disposition of the man whose promotion is in question. It is by merit that men rise in the service, a system which ensures that posts should only be assigned to the competent. . . .

This is the reason that they are successful in their undertakings, that they lord it over others, and are daily extending the bounds of their empire. These are not our ideas, with us there is no opening left for merit; birth is the standard for everything; the prestige of birth is the sole key to advancement in the public service.

—Ogier Ghiselin de Busbecq: Holy Roman Empire's ambassador to the Ottoman Court in his *The Turkish Letters*, 1555–1562

164. Which of the following is an underlying context for the legal status of the Janissaries described in the excerpt above?

(A) The Janissaries were free agents who sold their services to the highest bidder.

(B) The Janissaries were tied to the land and landowners but had some rights.

(C) The Janissaries were chattel slaves who were bought and sold to landowners.

(D) The Janissaries were the elite forces of the sultan but still under a form of servitude.

165. The formation of the Janissaries was part of a larger system of "collecting" young boys to serve the Ottoman state. Which of the following is the Turkish term for this system?

(A) Jizya

(B) Devshirme

(C) Jihad

(D) Mameluke

166. Stories exist of Christian families offering their sons to the Ottoman state in the hopes that they might become Janissaries. This was done primarily due to which of the following expectations?

(A) Social mobility

(B) Local famines

(C) Wars of conquest

(D) Monetary bribes

—Akbar greets two Jesuit priests in black robes in the meeting house in his capital at Fatehpur Sikri in 1603.

167. Based on the Persian miniature above, which of the following best shows the attitude of the Mughal emperor Akbar towards his non-Muslim subjects?

    (A) He imposed the jizya on his Hindu subjects.
    (B) He was interested in all religious faiths.
    (C) He destroyed their temples and taxed them.
    (D) He helped spread Hinduism to Southeast Asia.

168. In comparison to Akbar's meetings, his descendant Aurangzeb followed which religious policy in Mughal India?

    (A) He reimposed the jizya and religious intolerance.

    (B) He created a new religion that blended other faiths.

    (C) He added new innovations from Shia Islam.

    (D) He gradually drifted away from strict Islamic doctrine.

169. Mughal attitudes toward religion are best understood in the context of which of the following continuities of India?

    (A) The Mughals were visited by Christian missionaries.

    (B) The Mughal era saw the formation of the Sikh religion.

    (C) The Mughal entered India as seafaring merchants.

    (D) The Mughals ruled over a majority of non-Muslims.

When we arrived (at Calicut) they took us to a large church, and this is what we saw: The body of the church is as large as a monastery, all built of hewn stone and covered with tiles. At the main entrance rises a pillar of bronze as high as a mast, on the top of which was perched a bird, . . . In the centre of the body of the church rose a chapel, . . . Within this sanctuary stood a small image which they said represented Our Lady. Along the walls, by the main entrance, hung seven small bells. In this church the captain-major said his prayers, and we with him. We did not go within the chapel, for it is the custom that only certain servants of the church, called quasees, should enter. These quasees wore some threads passing over the left shoulder and under the right arm, in the same manner as our deacons wear the stole. They threw holy water over us, and gave us some white earth, which the Christians of this country are in the habit of putting on their foreheads, breasts, around the neck, and on the forearms. . . . Many other saints are painted on the walls of the church, wearing crowns. They were painted variously, with teeth protruding an inch from the mouth, and four or five arms.

—"Roteiro," a journal of Vasco da Gama's voyage written by an unknown member of the expedition.

170. From the excerpt above, which of the following is true?

   (A) DeGama and his men were overwhelmed by the exotic differences of India and Indians.

   (B) DeGama and his party mistook Hindus for Christians and a statue of an Indian deity for Mary.

   (C) DeGama and his force were attacked upon arrival and nearly wiped out.

   (D) DeGama naval fleet never made it past the port of Oran on the Arabian peninsula.

171. Which of the following acts best as a direct cause of the event described above?

   (A) The long-held European desire to reach India by an all-water route

   (B) The Iberian Christian reconquista against Andalusian Moors

   (C) The publication of Ibn Battuta's book in Northern European cities

   (D) The desire for new staple crops and tobacco from the Americas

172. The reference that "only certain servants of the church, called quasees, should enter" is referring to which group in Indian society?
    (A) Shudras
    (B) Kshatriyas
    (C) Brahmins
    (D) Vaishiyas

173. In contrast to the Portuguese arrival in India, the Spanish arrival in Americas was
    (A) Marked by cultural misunderstandings
    (B) Caused by a desire for trade with Asia
    (C) Done by long distance oceanic voyages
    (D) Resulted in conquest and settlement

—Early Indian matchlocks as illustrated in the "Baburnama" in the sixteenth century.

174. Which of the following represents a major change in South Asian governments ability to expand and dominate their empires in the Early Modern Era (1450–1750)?

(A) The use of stirrups and saddles
(B) The use of horses and chariots
(C) The use of gunpowder weapons
(D) The use of caravels and lateen sails

175. Which of the following represents a similarity among the nomadic Turkish tribes who later developed into the empires of the Ottomans, Mughals, and Safavids?

(A) Rule by a warrior class
(B) Adoption of shi'a islam
(C) Use of Jewish mercenaries
(D) Trade in tobacco products

O servant, where does thou seek Me? Lo! I am beside thee.

I am neither in temple nor in mosque: I am neither in Kaaba nor in Kailash. Neither am I in rites and ceremonies. . . . If thou are a true seeker, thou shalt at once see Me.

"It is needless to ask of a saint the caste to which he belongs. . . . The barber has sought God, the washerwoman, and the carpenter. . . .

Hindus and Muslims alike have achieved that End,

Where remains no mark of distinction.

—15th Century Indian poet and mystic, Kabir

176. Which of the following is true of the Bhakti movement based on the poem above?
   (A) It was strongly influenced by the new Sikh religion.
   (B) It was a Hindu attempt at accommodation with Islam.
   (C) It blended Chinese Confucianism with Indian Daoism.
   (D) It was the Indian version of the Wahhabi form of Islam.

177. Which of the following belief systems was a new religion from the Early Modern Era in South Asia that sought to navigate the differences between the Muslim rulers and the overwhelmingly Hindu majority?
   (A) Sikhism
   (B) Daoism
   (C) Wahabi
   (D) Jihad

—Taj Mahal, built during the Mughal era between 1631 and 1653. Frontal shot and detail.

178. Which of the following statements about the Taj Mahal is best supported by the images above?
   (A) It is a classic example of Islamic architecture.
   (B) It was used to house the royal Mughal family.
   (C) It acted as the Grand Bazaar for merchants.
   (D) It was built as a defensive fort against Hindus.

179. Similarly to the Palace of Versailles in France, the Taj Mahal

(A) Was later used to host numerous peace conferences
(B) Was used to demonstrate the power of the monarchs
(C) Was meant to be used as a royal mausoleum
(D) Was famed for its numerous bedrooms and galleries

180. Which of the following effects best captures the impact of the Mongol Empire on world history?

I. Spread of the bubonic plague across the Eurasian landmass
II. Stabilization of long-distance trade routes, which sparked greater demand for goods from distant lands
III. The exposure of old centers of civilization to new religious and intellectual trends

(A) I and II
(B) II and III
(C) I and III
(D) I, II, and III

181. Which of the following belief systems originated in India but was a minority faith by 1750?

(A) Hinduism
(B) Islam
(C) Janism
(D) Buddhism

182. Sikhs were first formed in the 15th century in northern India. Which of the following best demonstrates its main tenets?

(A) a syncretic faith which blends elements of Islam and Hinduism
(B) an Indian religion that stresses nonviolence and asceticism
(C) a holy order within the Catholic church that focused on education
(D) A philosophy that developed into a belief system later in China

183. Which destabilizing influence did the Ottoman, Mughal and Safavid empires face in the period 1450-1750?

(A) A growing influx of silver through trade with the West leading to widespread inflation
(B) Revived threats from Central Asian nomads
(C) Western siege and occupation of their capital cities
(D) Bubonic plague outbreaks that reduced populations by one-third

184. Which development in contemporary civilization had the greatest impact on the foreign relations of the Ottoman, Mughal and Safavid empires in the period 1450-1750?

(A) Drive of the Romanov dynasty in Russia for territorial expansion

(B) Mounting trade expeditions into the Indian Ocean basin launched by the Ming dynasty

(C) Flooding of global markets in precious metals through massive expansion of the gold-salt trade by West African kingdoms

(D) Movement of maritime West toward the core of a new global trade network

185. How did rulers of the Ottoman, Safavid and Mughal empires respond to the rising influence of the West in world affairs after 1500?

(A) A tendency to underestimate Western capacities led to failure to adopt Western military, technological and scientific advances

(B) Highly centralized drives to confront the West on the high seas thwarted Western encroachment on trade routes and port cities

(C) They pursued increased diplomatic and military dependence on Ming and Qing dynasties in China to organize resistance to Western domination

(D) Adoption of firearms and artillery enabled coordinated assaults on the homelands of the Western merchants

186. Religious tolerance, Hindu-Muslim intermarriage and abolition of the jizya head tax are all amost closely associated with which Mughal ruler?

(A) Babur

(B) Akbar

(C) Auranzeb

(D) Shah Jahan

187. Which three Muslim empires emerged from the wreckage left behind after the Mongol invasions?

(A) Umayyad, Safavid, Mughal

(B) Mughal, Safavid, Ottoman

(C) Abbasid, Ottoman, Umayyad

(D) Mughal, Umayyad, Abbasid

188. Which statement best characterizes power relations among the centers of Eurasian civilizations as they approached the year 1450?

(A) Islamic caliphates are reaching the height of their power and influence.

(B) Ming rulers of China have redoubled their efforts to move to the center of maritime trading networks in the East Asian and Indian Ocean.

(C) A power vacuum of sorts has opened, as Byzantine, Abbasid, and Ming Chinese powers become less of a force in global affairs.

(D) Western Europe dominates world trade.

189. Which Western power established trade forts at crucial locations in the Indian Ocean basin including Ormuz, Goa, and Malacca in the early sixteenth century?

(A) Spain

(B) England

(C) Netherlands

(D) Portugal

—World map showing trade-winds by Edmond Halley, 1686

190. The wind currents shown in the map above were used to great effect during which period of long-distance trade and interaction in world history?

(A) The Crusades
(B) The Age of Exploration
(C) The Peopling of Oceania
(D) The Mongol Expansion

191. The trade winds in the Indian Ocean contributed most directly to which of the following

(A) The spread of Buddhism to the East African coast in the tenth century
(B) The existence of steam technology in navigation during the eighteenth century
(C) The monsoon winds that provided needed water for South Asian agriculture
(D) The use of irrigation canals in ancient Egypt to create surplus crops

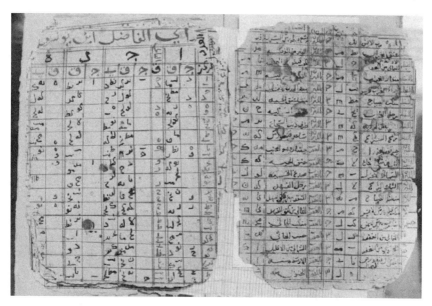

—A manuscript page from the African city of Timbuktu showing a table
of astronomical information. Early Modern Era (1450–1750).

192. Which of the following explains the importance of astronomy in the
Islamic world?

(A) Horoscopes are needed for the pilgrimage to Medina.
(B) Knowledge of astronomy is important for daily prayer.
(C) There is great respect for medical knowledge.
(D) Celestial wonders are considered good luck for trade.

193. By 1200, Baghdad's House of Wisdom, European universities and
Timbuktu were similar for being important centers of which of the
following?

(A) Trade
(B) Learning
(C) Transportation
(D) Islam

The inhabitants of this country are tawny-colored. Their food is confined to the flesh of seals, whales and gazelles, and the roots of herbs. They are dressed in skins, and wear sheaths over their virile members. They are armed with poles of olive wood to which a horn, browned in the fire, is attached. Their numerous dogs resemble those of Portugal, and bark like them. The birds of the country, likewise, are the same as in Portugal, and include cormorants, gulls, turtle doves, crested larks, and many others. The climate is healthy and temperate, and produces good herbage. On the day after we had cast anchor, that is to say on Thursday (November 9), we landed with the captain-major, and made captive one of the natives, who was small of stature. . . . He was taken on board the captain-major's ship, and being placed at table he ate of all we ate. On the following day the captain-major had him well dressed and sent ashore.

On the following day (November 10) fourteen or fifteen natives came to where our ship lay. The captain-major landed and showed them a variety of merchandise, with the view of finding out whether such things were to be found in their country. This merchandise included cinnamon, cloves, seed-pearls, gold, and many other things, but it was evident that they had no knowledge whatever of such articles, and they were consequently given round bells and tin rings. This happened on Friday, and the like took place on Saturday.

—An account of Vasco Da Gama along the shore of Africa, 1497–1498.

194. The account of Vasco Da Gama in Africa is similar to Europeans experiences in the Americans in that?

(A) They both used Swahili language translators to conduct negotiations.
(B) They both show societies that were governed by democratic principles.
(C) They both had no domesticated animals that could be used for labor.
(D) They both show the relative isolation from the larger interconnected world.

195. Which of the following explains why the African natives were asked about cinnamon, cloves, and gold?

(A) Europeans were primarily interested in commercial opportunities.
(B) Europeans were motivated by religious motives to spread Christianity.
(C) Europeans were conducting scientific surveys of the flora and fauna.
(D) Europeans were interested in feeding the hungry Africans.

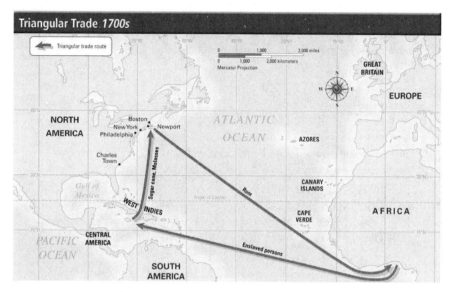

Trade routes involving the enslavement of Africans.

196. A historian would most likely use the map above in studying which of the following?

(A) Immigration patterns around the world
(B) Triangular trade network across the Atlantic
(C) Industrialization across the Americas
(D) The market for luxury goods in Asia

197. Which is most true of the Middle Passage?

(A) It was generally a pleasant voyage and the slaves were well cared for.
(B) Mortality on the ships was high, so slaves were overpacked to offset losses.
(C) It generally lasted a year or more depending on the monsoon winds.
(D) African naval expertise was key to guiding vessels across the Atlantic.

198. Compared to the Indian Ocean slave trade, the Atlantic slave trade, differed in that

(A) Slaves were not exchanged for trade goods but tribute.
(B) It offered little social advancement for slaves.
(C) It was larger in scale, greater in profit and mortality.
(D) Was of shorter duration but longer in distance.

199. Which of the following does NOT belong in a list of factors preventing European powers from establishing anything more than a limited coastal settlement on the African continent in the period 1450–1750?

(A) Climate
(B) Disease
(C) Impassable rivers
(D) Inferior weapons

200. Which would be the LEAST typical trade transaction along Africa's northeast coast in the period 1450–1750?

(A) Ivory exported to India
(B) Gold exported to Persia
(C) Female slaves exported to Arabian peninsula for domestic labor
(D) Female slaves exported to a West Indies sugar plantation

201. The Afrikaners who settled in southern Africa traced their origin back to which European region?

(A) England
(B) Germany
(C) Netherlands
(D) France

202. In which regional waterways did the West most rapidly emerge into a dominant position after 1450?

(A) Eastern Mediterranean
(B) South China Sea
(C) Arabian Sea
(D) Caribbean Sea

—Cortez and La Malinche meet Moctezuma II, 1519, from the "Lienzo de Tlaxcala," which was created by the Tlaxcalans to remind the Spanish of their loyalty to Castile and the importance of Tlaxcala during the Conquest. circa 1550.

203. The image above shows evidence of which continuity in Latin American diplomatic relations?
   (A) Tribute from conquered peoples
   (B) Legalese diplomatic language
   (C) Female translators
   (D) Ritual bowing

204. The presence of Malinche, as a Tlaxcalan translator for the Spanish is a reminder of which essential fact in the success of the conquistadores in the early 1500s?
   (A) The Aztecs and the Spanish had a patriarchal society.
   (B) Lack of immunity in Amerindians played a key role.
   (C) Native American allies were vital in the Spanish victory.
   (D) The use of wind currents in sea battles against the Aztecs.

—Virgin Mary of the Rich Mountain (Potosi) "Bolivia". (17th to 18th century).

205. The image of Christianity's Virgin Mary imposed onto the mountain in Potosi in Bolivia is an example of which historical process?

(A) Syncretism
(B) Assimilation
(C) Conquest
(D) Trade

206. The expression in Spanish "vale un Potosí", meaning "to be of great value" refers to the mountain in Bolivia which was famous in the Early Modern Era for which resource?

(A) Gold
(B) Silver
(C) Copper
(D) Tin

—Casta painting showing a mixed race man "Mestizo" with an Indigenous Native American "Indian" woman with mixed race children who were referred to as "coyote."

207. The image above can be best understood in the context of which historical event?

(A) The Spanish and Portuguese conquest of the Americas
(B) The capture of slaves in the interior of the African continent
(C) The nineteenth-century Latin American independence movements
(D) The Reconquista in the Iberian Peninsula by Christian forces

208. The image above best demonstrates which of the following conclusions about Colonial Latin America in the 1500s to 1800s era?

(A) Strong industrial base and infrastructure
(B) A predominantly Christian populace
(C) A decline in agriculture and trade
(D) Sharp racial and class divisions

The Caribbean was the first region in the Americas to receive African slaves via the transatlantic trade. The Spanish crown subsidized the slave traffic to the island settlements in Cuba, Puerto Rico and Santo Domingo in the early sixteenth century, seeking to stimulate a sugar plantation economy much like those that the Iberians had implanted in the eastern Atlantic islands in the late Middle Ages. The Spanish experiment with slaving and sugar planting was short-lived, even though sugar and slavery never completely disappeared from those islands. None the less, it was not until the mid-seventeenth century when English colonists in Barbados made the transition from tobacco and cotton to sugar planting that the Caribbean became a major site in the Atlantic plantation complex and, along with Brazil, the chief American destination for enslaved African workers. Over the next 200 years, the fortunes of different islands and empires waxed and waned in the Caribbean but slavery and slave trading persisted.

—*Caribbean Emancipation* by Christopher Schmidt-Nowara, 2011.

209. Which of the following provides the historical context for the use of African labor, European markets, and a New World crop as discussed in the secondary source above?

(A) The Scientific Revolution
(B) The Commercial Revolution
(C) The Green Revolution
(D) The French Revolution

210. Which economic system was in place when the exchange of goods discussed in the excerpt above arose?

(A) European mercantilist laws
(B) Laissez-faire principles
(C) Renaissance guild by-laws
(D) Medieval manorialism

211. To which location was the greatest number of enslaved Africans transported?

(A) Spanish Mexico
(B) Portuguese Brazil
(C) British North America
(D) Dutch Indonesia

212. Which impulse for the colonization of North America was generally missing from the colonization of the rest of the New World?
    (A) Setting up slave plantations
    (B) The search for gold
    (C) Freedom from religious persecution
    (D) Expansion of royal authority

213. In which colonized region of the globe did Western cultural practices supplant existing cultural practices most completely after 1450?
    (A) West Africa
    (B) North and South America
    (C) East Asia
    (D) South Asia

214. In which way did the Spanish colonies reproduce existing Iberian social structures?
    (A) Colonies were established as monarchies in their own right.
    (B) Gender roles were preserved from the very start as equal proportions of Spanish males and females settled the New World.
    (C) Peninsulares sought to reproduce essentially feudal estates with indigenous labor filling the role of the Spanish serf.
    (D) Religious tolerance remained an important factor in integrating diverse peoples into a cohesive social unit.

215. Which New World commodity was of the greatest value to the Portuguese monarchy in the early phases of the settlement of Brazil?
    (A) Potato
    (B) Tomato
    (C) Silver
    (D) Sugar

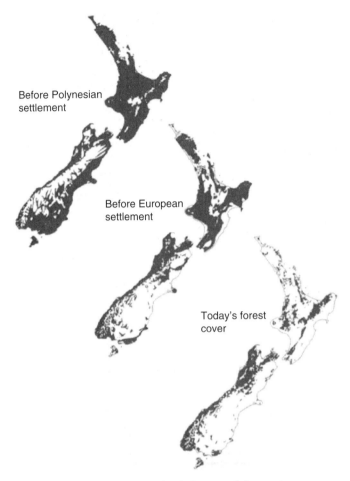

Before Polynesian settlement

Before European settlement

Today's forest cover

—Maps of New Zealand showing deforestation

216. The image above show clear evidence of which of the following?

(A) The harmful impact of human settlement
(B) The effect of trade winds on seashores
(C) The damage done by seagull nesting
(D) Rainfall levels between the islands

217. Which of the following peoples first settled in New Zealand starting in 1200?

(A) Europeans
(B) Swahili
(C) Polynesians
(D) Aborigines

—*School of Athens* by the artist, Raphael, circa 1509 to 1511.

218. Which of the following breakthrough artistic technique is utilized in the painting?
(A) The use of the pyramid configuration
(B) Vanishing lines of perspective
(C) Egg yolks as a base for paints
(D) Painting on wet plaster or frescoes

219. Which of the following is a philosophical change during this time that acts as context for the painting?
(A) The increased use of secular and non-religious themes
(B) The decline of preclassical thought
(C) The rise of a courtier class that espoused Chivalric ideals
(D) A decrease in Egyptian and Mesopotamian deities

I disagree very much with those who are unwilling that Holy Scripture, translated into the vulgar tongue, be read by the uneducated, as if Christ himself taught such intricate doctrines that they could scarcely be understood by very few theologians, or as if the strength of the Christian religion consisted in men's ignorance of it...I would that even the lowliest women read the Gospels and the Pauline Epistles. And I would that they were translated into all languages so that they could be read and understood not only by Scots and Irish but also by Turks and Saracens. . . . Would that, as a result, the farmer sing some portion of them at the plow, the weaver hum some parts of them to the movement of his shuttle, the traveler lighten the weariness of the journey with stories of this kind!

—Erasmus of Rotterdam, 1529

220. The above passage clearly shows the influence of which of the following upon Christian theological trends?
    (A) Renaissance humanism
    (B) Enlightenment ideas about rationality
    (C) Catholic dogmatic traditions
    (D) Medieval scholasticism

221. Which of the following best demonstrates the cause for the historical situation in the reading above?
    (A) An increase in spoken languages
    (B) An increase in literacy and printing
    (C) A decrease in Medieval scholarship
    (D) A slow decline in the use of English

—"Peasant Dance" by Pieter Breughel

222. The painting above is typical of the Northern Renaissance in that

(A) It supported the papacy during the Reformation.

(B) It focused on everyday issues and secular concerns.

(C) It had bright colors and was painted on canvas.

(D) It celebrated religious festivals and ceremonies.

223. Which of the following is true of most peasants in Western European societies?

(A) They suffered under harsh conditions since the Postclassical Era.

(B) They rose in the social structure above merchants and traders.

(C) Their lives began to improve with the end of the Black Death.

(D) They were subject to conscription into the Czar's armed forces.

—Luther Before the Diet of Worms, 1521, painted by Anton von Werner

224. The image depicts Martin Luther answering to Holy Roman Emperor Charles V. Which relationship between church and state best describes Catholic Western Europe in the early modern Era?

    (A) Rulers created new religions to unify conquered peoples.

    (B) Popes asserted that royal laws were superior to divine laws.

    (C) Rulers deferred to secular authorities in regulating heresy.

    (D) Rulers had a symbiotic close relationship with religious authorities.

225. Martin Luther's popularity and survival was due in large part to which of the following factors?

    (A) Printing press technology

    (B) Black Death/bubonic plague

    (C) Gold imports from the Americas

    (D) Roman Catholic reforms

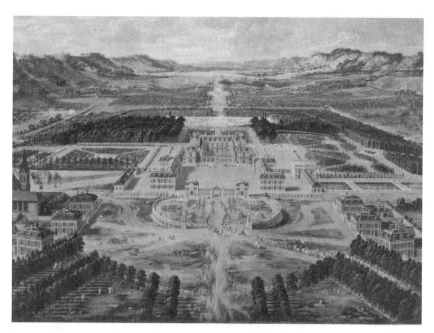

—1668 Painting of Versailles showing the palace, gardens, and fountains.

The visits of Louis XIV becoming more frequent, he enlarged the château by degrees till its immense buildings afforded better accommodation for the Court than was to be found at St. Germain, where most of the courtiers had to put up with uncomfortable lodgings in the town. The Court was therefore removed to Versailles in 1682, not long before the Queen's death. The new building contained an infinite number of rooms for courtiers, and the King liked the grant of these rooms to be regarded as a coveted privilege.

He availed himself of the frequent festivities at Versailles, and his excursions to other places, as a means of making the courtiers assiduous in their attendance and anxious to please him; for he nominated beforehand those who were to take part in them, and could thus gratify some and inflict a snub on others.

—San Simon on life at Versailles

226. Which of the following best explains why rulers continue to use monumental architecture during the period from 1450 to 1750?

(A) To celebrate their coronations

(B) To create a gathering places for worship

(C) To legitimize their rule and authority

(D) To provide jobs for the masses

227. Which of the following terms best describes the form of government practiced by the French King, Louis XIV?

(A) Constitutional monarchy

(B) Absolute monarchy

(C) Totalitarian dictatorship

(D) Parliamentary mandate

—Print showing the French King, Louis XIV, visiting the Academy of the Sciences in 1671

228. Based on the image above, which of the following was a cause of the Scientific Revolution in Europe during the seventeenth and eighteenth centuries?

(A) Royal patronage and support
(B) The trial of Galileo Galilei
(C) The backing of the Pope
(D) The spread of gunpowder

229. Compared to the result depicted in the image above, a Scientific Revolution did NOT come to Asia because of which of the following?

(A) Asia was completely isolated from West and refrained from trade and contact.

(B) Asia had little experience with literacy and lacked an educated scholar class.

(C) Asian monarchs were primarily interested in conquest and less in art and science.

(D) Intellectual curiosity was being stifled by a strict adherence to belief systems.

230. Which of the following does NOT belong in a list of Catholic doctrines rejected by Martin Luther?

(A) Papal authority

(B) Granting of indulgences

(C) Monasticism

(D) Acceptance of the Holy Trinity

231. Compared, broadly speaking, with other centers of civilization in the world, which of the following had become the most distinctive characteristic of Western intellectual life by about 1750?

(A) Concern with manipulation of nature to serve human interests

(B) Centrality of science in understanding reality

(C) Appreciation of poetry in elite circles

(D) Importance of the written word in preservation of the wisdom of the past

232. Which group suffered the greatest loss of authority as absolute monarchy took hold in the West beginning in the seventeenth century?

(A) Monarchs

(B) Merchants

(C) Peasants

(D) Aristocrats

233. Which of the following kingdoms serves as an exception to the rule of the growing power of absolute monarchies in the West in the period 1450–1750?

(A) Spain

(B) France

(C) Austria-Hungary

(D) England

—"Standing on the Ugra River," 1480. Miniature in Russian chronicle. XVI century. "And our men had beaten many foes with arrows and muskets, and their arrows had fallen between our men, and had nobody hurting, and had repelling them off the shore."

234. Which of the following acts as context for the image on the previous page on Russia in the Early Modern Era (1450–1750)?

(A) The extension of the Silk Road into Russia

(B) The rise of the Russian czsars and state

(C) The decline of serfdom in European Russia

(D) The use of the rivers as conduits for trade

235. Based on the image on the previous page and the brief text, which technology had diffused to the Russian state by the 15th century?

(A) Navigational

(B) Bow and arrow

(C) Gunpowder

(D) Steam power

In the year 1497, in the month of September, the Grand Prince of all Rus' Ivan Vasilievic, with his children and boyars, compiled a code of law on how boyars and major-domos (okolnichii) are to administer justice.

Article 8. And if evidence is brought against anyone of theft, brigandage, murder, false accusation, or any other such evil deed, and he is a notorious criminal, then the boyar is to order him executed and the sum at issue paid from his property, and whatever remains of this property shall be taken by the boyar and his secretary for themselves.

Article 57. And peasants may leave a canton [to go to another canton], or [go] from village to village, once a year, for a week before and a week after St. George's Day in the autumn.

—The Sudebnik was the legal code of Russia, passed in 1497.

236. The code of laws above show a large degree of autonomy for Russian nobles, the boyars. This was probably due to which factor?

(A) Russia's tradition of liberal light-handed government

(B) Russia's trust in its tradition and religions

(C) Russia's lack of warm water ports and harbors

(D) Russia's immense size and difficulty of governing

237. One theory for the continuation of serfdom in Russia whereas it had largely died out in Western Europe has to do with

(A) Its vast size yet relatively small population led to a need to control serfs as a source of labor.

(B) Serfs were originally from Southern Europe and the popularity of scientific racism hardened attitudes towards them.

(C) The end of the Silk Road trade made agriculture more important and serfs were now being sold for money.

(D) Russia borrowed many Mongol ideas and the Mongols convinced peasants to become serfs.

—Woodcut of Czar Peter the Great shearing off the beard of a noble.

238. Czar Peter was opposed to nobles having beards. He felt they were in opposition to which of the following changes, he trying to institute in Russia?

(A) Technology
(B) Modernization
(C) Centralization
(D) Expansion

239. Which of the following items of clothing or appearance was NOT seen by various governments in world history as oppositional to change?

(A) Shaved heads and pigtails during the Qing dynasty
(B) Brimmed hats during Ataturk's reign in Turkey
(C) Powdered wigs during the French Revolution
(D) Wearing samurai swords in Meiji Japan

240. How did Russia tend to fit into the emerging global economy in the period 1450–1750?

(A) As a source of serf labor transported to till the soils of Western Europe

(B) As a market for grain grown in the New World

(C) As the primary Old World destination of the silver being taken out of the New World

(D) As a supplier of grain, timber, fur, and other raw materials to the West

241. In which neighboring region(s) did the Russian Empire gain the most land during the Romanov dynasty?

(A) Poland

(B) Baltic States

(C) Black Sea region

(D) Siberia and Central Asia

242. The shift of the Russian imperial capital to which city indicated a shift in orientation toward the West under the rule of Peter the Great?

(A) St. Petersburg

(B) Moscow

(C) Kiev

(D) Vladivostok

243. Which of the following best describes the attitude of Peter and Catherine the Great toward adopting change along Western lines?

(A) It was a waste of time and an insult to Russian tradition.

(B) Its harmless influence was allowed to spread without interference.

(C) It was a source of new ideas and methods to increase the power of the ruling family at home and abroad.

(D) It was a key step on the road to Russian democracy.

In October 1679, Frederick Philipse shipped the following ship cargo from Manhattan to Amsterdam on board *The Charles*.	In May 1680, *The Charles* returned to Manhattan with a ship cargo to New York, which included the following items.
2345 beaver skins 2694 small furs 14 cat skins 104 black bear skins 1355 fox skins 438 otter skins 1382 raccoon skins 512 cow skins (in the hair) 181 hogsheads (large barrels) of Maryland tobacco 166 sticks of Honduras logwood	55 coils of heavy rope 538 pair of Wadmoll stockings 1494 rolls of Holland cloth 20 dozen pewter spoons 209 gun barrels 18 cases of window glass 725 drinking glasses 18 dozen spectacles 290 iron pots 503 gross of tobacco pipes 200 cases of nails 22 shovels 10 pieces of colored calico cloth

°Ship ledgers of the Dutch ship, *The Charles*.

244. The goods listed above are best described as which of the following pairs?

(A) Raw materials/manufactured goods
(B) Animals products/metal products
(C) Of American origin/of Asian origin
(D) Factory goods/unfinished goods

245. The goods listed to and from the colony of Manhattan and Amsterdam above demonstrate which of the following economic practices/theories?

(A) Communism
(B) The guild system
(C) Capitalism
(D) Mercantilism

—Caravel ship.

246. Ships such as the one in the image were most likely to be financed or backed by

(A) Wealthy individual investors
(B) Joint stock companies
(C) Piracy and theft
(D) Letters of marque

247. Which of the following was NOT a technological innovation in the Iberian ship development in the 15th and 16th century?

(A) Stern post rudder
(B) Lateen sails
(C) Deep water hulls
(D) Multiple ranks of oars

248. What was the demographic impact of the Columbian Exchange on the populations of the Old World?

(A) Population growth across the Old World based on New World crops such as corn and the potato

(B) Massive depopulation of Western Europe due to migration to the Americas

(C) Sharp increase in the West African population to furnish individuals for the slave trade

(D) Sharp decrease in male populations as many sailors died at sea

249. Which of the following established a line of demarcation separating Spanish and Portuguese claims in the New World?

(A) Treaty of Versailles

(B) Edict of Nantes

(C) Treaty of Westphalia

(D) Treaty of Tordesillas

CHAPTER 3

The Modern Era: 1750 to 1900

Controlling Idea: The Long 19th Century

Historians have written of the Long 19th Century, from 1750 to 1914 but recently cut down to 1900. This dynamic period has seen two major revolutions: one economic in the industrial revolution and the second, political in a series of revolutions. Originally limited to a core in the Western world, it soon spread out to all corners of the globe that were first exposed in the previous era. In 1750 the Industrial Revolution was in its infancy and did not shape life in a significant way outside the West and its New World colonies. By 1900 there was not a corner of the globe that had not been impacted by the growth of this dynamic new economic force. This change was most visible in the new technology and has transformed societies. This change also coincided and was impacted by and helped cause waves of migration from both rural to urban and across oceans generally from the Old World to the New World. Industrialization was also, symbiotic with the rise of capitalism. This era also soon saw challenges to capitalism in unions and new ideas of socialism and communism. The political corollary of these economic changes was that the old feudal and monarchical systems of ruler were overthrown and undermined in a series of events that took off on a global scale in the wake of the French Revolution. The long 19th century continued with the spread of more widespread beliefs or "isms" such as nationalism and feminism.

 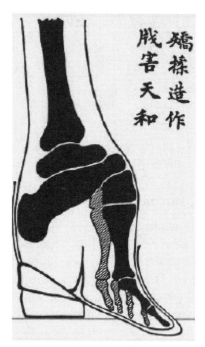

—Chinese girl with bound feet

250. Which of the following conclusions is best supported by the two images above?

(A) Chinese society supported female empowerment

(B) Chinese society was heavily influenced by Vietnam

(C) Chinese society was a strict patriarchy

(D) Chinese society practiced Social Darwinism

251. The practice of foot-binding diminished in China during the late 19th and early 20th centuries. Which of the following had the greatest impact on its ending?

(A) Japanese imperialists

(B) American merchants

(C) Daoist monks

(D) Western missionaries

When Chinese civilization encounters a barbarian people, those bar-barians are transformed by Chinese ways into a civilized people. Barbarians look up to China and are delighted to receive its civi-lizing influence. This is the way things are in the natural order of things. This is the way human beings ought to feel. China is like the roots of a plant supplying nourishment for the branches and le aves. It is like the hands and feet that protect the belly and chest of the human body. This should never change . . . .

These Europeans come from a land far away from China, so it is only natural that their customs are quite different from Chinese customs. . . .

However, unfortunately the world is such a big place that Europe had no contact with China for quite a long time. . . .

That meant that, regrettably, Europe was not introduced to the basic principles of the Great Way, and Europeans were not turned into more virtuous people by its civilizing power. Europe has instead been saturated with a lot of misleading notions, and Europeans as a result tend to spout a bunch of nonsense, criticizing the teach-ings of the earlier Confucian sages and condemning the teachings of later Neo-Confucian philosophers. It appears to be next to impos-sible to awaken those men to their true inner nature and get them to change their mistaken practices. Europeans do have a re markable talent for technology. They easily surpass the Chinese in that area. But that achievement makes them arrogant, and they think that they can convert the whole world to their way of thinking. They need to think again!

—Korean scholar, Yi Hangno (1792–1868)
"Sinifying the Western Barbarians."

252. Which of the following explains why Yi Hangno held such attitudes?

(A) Korea was a country with a long Chinese influence.

(B) Confucianism, like China's writing system, was rejected.

(C) Korea was colonized by Japan in the sixteenth century.

(D) Korea sent educational missions to Germany and France.

253. According to the text, the cause of the lack of interaction between Europe and China is due to

(A) Warfare

(B) Geography

(C) Philosophy

(D) Belief systems

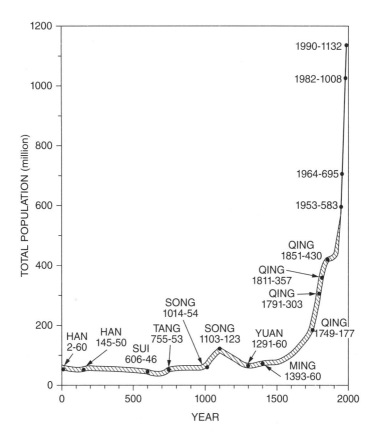

254. Which of the following best supports a historical argument for the huge population growth illustrated in the chart during the Qing Dynasty from 1644 to 1911?

(A) New World crops
(B) Gunpowder technology
(C) Domestication of animals
(D) Silk Road trade

255. Which of the following resulted from the big jump in China's population during the Qing dynasty (1644–1911)?

(A) A strict ban on polygamy as a way to increase the number of available brides
(B) A steady migration from China to areas like the Americas and South East Asia
(C) A one-child policy for each married couple in the People's Republic of China
(D) The formation of state education for each child born in China before 1911

—The British warship *Nemesis* destroying Chinese war junks during the Second Battle of Chuenpi, 1841.

256. The image above is best understood in the context of
    (A) The Taiping Rebellion
    (B) The Macartney mission
    (C) Meiji Restoration
    (D) The Opium War

257. Which was a direct result of the historical event depicted above?
    (A) The island of Hong Kong became a British colony.
    (B) The port of Yokohama was opened to trade.
    (C) The Russians were forced to pay an indemnity.
    (D) Korea was put under Japanese protection.

China: The Cake of Kings . . . and Emperors, in Le Petit Journal, 1898

258. Which of the following contributed most directly to the condition depicted in the cartoon above?

(A) China's total isolation from the rest of the world

(B) China's military weakness compared to the West

(C) China's dynastic cycle guaranteed transition to a ruling elite capable of halting Western imperial designs on China

(D) China's trade imbalance with Japan and the West

259. China's condition in the cartoon above question 258 is best compared to the situation in which of the following areas of the world in the late nineteenth and early twentieth century?

(A) Africa
(B) Western Europe
(C) United States of America
(D) Eastern Europe

260. Based on the image above, why is Japan seated at the table instead of being a victim itself of being cut into pieces?

(A) Japan modernized and strengthened itself through the Meiji reforms.
(B) Western nations were not interested in Japan due to its small size.
(C) Japan had not opened itself to outside influences yet by 1898.
(D) By 1898 Japan had already defeated Britain and France in war.

261. Which of the following best describes China's trade relations with the rest of the world by about 1750?

(A) Export of Chinese manufactured and luxury goods in exchange for Western manufactured and luxury goods
(B) Export of Chinese manufactured and luxury goods in exchange for silver
(C) Import of Western manufactured and luxury goods in exchange for silver
(D) Negligible levels of trade with the rest of the world since China produced all it needed

262. Which of the following best explains the reason the British turned to trading opium in China?

(A) First hand experience supplying mass opium addiction in the thirteen colonies proved the profitability of the trade.
(B) British merchants could find no other commodity the Chinese needed.
(C) Successful expansion of the opium trade in India provided a model for replication.
(D) Imperialist designs for direct rule in China would be more easily attainable over a population pacified by narcotics.

263. Which of the following does NOT belong in a list of policies generally followed by a rising Chinese dynasty according to the Mandate of Heaven?

(A) Repair and expansion of dams, canals, and roads

(B) Lowering tax burdens for the peasantry

(C) Expanding opportunities for peasants to own land

(D) Concentration of land ownership into ever fewer hands

264. Which statement best captures the ruling Qing dynasty's attitude toward the West particularly in the period before the Opium Wars?

(A) Western civilization possessed military and industrial practices worthy of emulation.

(B) Western civilization posed a mortal threat to Chinese civilization.

(C) Western civilization was just another barbarian foreign society.

(D) Western civilization possessed artistic and intellectual practices worthy of emulation.

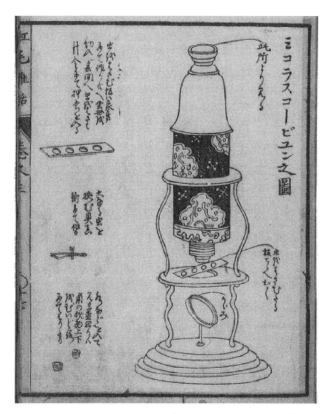

—Illustration of a microscope in a 1787 book, *Various Accounts from the Dutch*.

265. The image above is proof of which of the following truths of Japanese isolation?

(A) It was absolute with zero contact between Japan and the outside world.

(B) It was never total isolation and a small but important stream of information came through Nagasaki.

(C) The Japanese learned more from China during the Tokugawa era than earlier eras.

(D) The Japanese were only interested in religious and other cultural Western influences.

266. Which types of information from the outside world were Japan and China most interested in attaining?

(A) Religious and cultural

(B) Linguistic and social

(C) Scientific and technical

(D) Governmental and diplomatic

GREAT AND GOOD FRIEND: I send you this public letter by Commodore Matthew C. Perry, an officer of the highest rank in the navy of the United States, and commander of the squadron now visiting your imperial majesty's dominions.

I have directed Commodore Perry to assure your imperial majesty that I entertain the kindest feelings toward your majesty's person and government, and that I have no other object in sending him to Japan but to propose to your imperial majesty that the United States and Japan should live in friendship and have commercial intercourse with each other.

The Constitution and laws of the United States forbid all interference with the religious or political concerns of other nations. I have particularly charged Commodore Perry to abstain from every act which could possibly disturb the tranquility of your imperial majesty's dominions.

The United States of America reach from ocean to ocean, and our Territory of Oregon and State of California lie directly opposite to the dominions of your imperial majesty. Our steamships can go from California to Japan in eighteen days. . . .

I am desirous that our two countries should trade with each other, for the benefit both of Japan and the United States. We know that the ancient laws of your imperial majesty's government do not allow of foreign trade, except with the Chinese and the Dutch; but as the state of the world changes and new governments are formed, it seems to be wise, from time to time, to make new laws. There was a time when the ancient laws of your imperial majesty's government were first made.

. . .

I have sent Commodore Perry, with a powerful squadron, to pay a visit to your imperial majesty's renowned city of Yedo: friendship, commerce, a supply of coal and provisions, and protection for our shipwrecked people.

May the Almighty have your imperial majesty in His great and holy keeping!

. . . Your good friend, MILLARD FILLMORE

267. This letter by US president Fillmore is addressed to "his imperial majesty" in Japan. This indicates which of the following statements about US knowledge of Japan in the 1850s?
    (A) They were very respectful and tried to adhere to Confucian notions of propriety and diplomacy.
    (B) They failed to understand that Japan was a tributary nation to China, similar to how Korea and Vietnam were tribute states.
    (C) They were unaware that the Japanese emperor was a figurehead and that the Shogun actually rules the nation.
    (D) They believed that the Japanese emperor were direct descendants of the sun-goddess Amaterasu.

268. Which of the following was a direct result of the visit of US Commodore Mathew Perry to Japan in 1854?

(A) Japan opened up and soon sent diplomatic missions to Western nations.

(B) Japan reverted to its samurai tradition and fought losing battles to stay isolated.

(C) Japan chose to only open up to the Russians and signed a treaty in Hokkaido.

(D) Japan increased some trade but resisted US efforts at diplomatic relations.

—Steam train between Tokyo and Yokohama by HIroshige, 1875.

269. Which of the following events was most important in creating the economic conditions illustrated in the image above?

(A) The Tokugawa Shogun's decision to isolate itself from the world in 1613

(B) U.S. Navy commodore Mathew Perry's visit to Tokyo Bay in 1853

(C) The Chinese acceptance of the Treaty of Nanking in 1842 to open more trade ports

(D) The Japanese seizure of Korea and Taiwan in the Sino-Japanese war in 1895

270. Compared to the changes in Japan shown in the image above by the late nineteenth century China

(A) Largely did not reform its society and economy

(B) Surpassed Japan in reforming its society and economy

(C) Had still not opened its nation to foreign trade and influence

(D) Had only reformed its economy but not its politics or society

271. The Japanese woodblock print above question 269 was produced in a domestic system with specialized labor with a breakdown of labor tasks. This was part of a Japanese tradition that stretched back to before the Tokugawa era. Which of the following therefore is true?

(A) Japan's belief system had switched to the monotheistic faith of Christianity.

(B) Japan's artistic tradition had long surpassed the West in its use of colors and detail.

(C) Japan's society held merchants and craftsmen in the highest regard and status.

(D) Japan's modernization had some antecedents before the encounter with the West in 1853.

The money that a factory girl earned was often more than a farmer's income for the entire year. For these rural families, the girls were an invaluable source of income. The poor peasants during this period had to turn over 60 percent of their crops to the landlord. Thus the poor peasants had only bits of rice mixed with weeds for food. The peasants' only salvation was the girls who went to work in the factories.

—Buddhist priest from a rural area on textile workers in Japan, circa 1900.

272. Compared to the situation in the excerpt, mechanization of the cotton textile industry in Western nations was similar in that they

(A) Relied exclusively on believers in Buddhism

(B) Relied on generous government financing

(C) Relied on a rice based diet for workers

(D) Relied heavily on female labor from rural areas

273. A historian studying Japanese industrialization would most likely find this account useful as a source of information because?

(A) Buddhism has been a popular religion in Japan for centuries.

(B) The priest was from an area that recruited these workers.

(C) The landlords and factory owners were often the same individuals.

(D) The Buddhist clergy encouraged the monastic lifestyle for women.

274. How was the opening of Japan to the West different from other encounters between majors civilizations and the West around the world to the period 1750–1900?

(A) French imperialists who dominated Japan refused to confer citizenry on the Japanese as they had in Africa.

(B) Japanese ruling elites remained in continuous control of the pace and terms of relations with the West.

(C) Japan was the only civilization whose first contact with the West was with the United States.

(D) Exposure of the Japanese to Christianity created a minority community that assisted in direct colonial rule by the British.

275. Which of the following best describes the political system set up in Japan during the Meiji Restoration?

(A) Proletarian dictatorship

(B) Democratic republic

(C) Constitutional monarchy

(D) Feudal state

276. How did industrial development in Japan and Russia tend to differ from similar processes in Western Europe and the United States?

(A) Industrial development tended to be more state-directed

(B) Industrial development was not applied to military purposes

(C) Industrial development did not spur territorial expansion

(D) Industrial development was more dependent on immigrant labor

277. In which area did westernization of Japan have the least impact?

(A) Politics

(B) Religion

(C) Economy

(D) Fashion

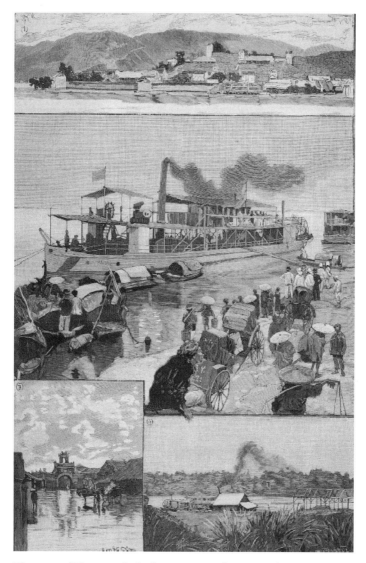

—The port of Hanoi in Indochina in 1891 from French newspaper *Le Monde* illustrated.

278. In the French newspaper image above, which of the following demonstrates continuity in Southeast Asia in the era of 1750–1900?

(A) The use of conical straw hats, carrying poles, and rickshaws

(B) The use of steam-powered riverboats and rickshaws

(C) The importation of European manufactured goods

(D) The building of French government buildings

279. The image above is similar to other Asian port cities such as Shanghai, Kobe, and Manilla in which of the following areas?

(A) These port cities were all part of French colonies since the eighteenth century.

(B) These areas of the world were intensely connected to the world commerce.

(C) These ports all used sail boats and other older means of transportation.

(D) The local people were opposed to trade and interaction with Europe.

280. How did the Dutch gain control of Java?

(A) Massive emigration from the Netherlands to Indonesia gave the Dutch a demographic advantage.

(B) Rapid industrialization and urbanization allowed for management of the majority of the population at work and at home.

(C) Shrewd exploitation of existing political divisions on the island resulted in territorial concessions.

(D) Supremacy in military technology resulted in direct rule after an initial period of warfare.

—Napoleon and his generals in Egypt.

281. Which of the following was a result of Napoleon's invasion of Egypt in 1798?

(A) It broke away from the Ottoman Empire.

(B) It was reconquered by Mameluke forces.

(C) India was lost as a British colony forever.

(D) The Ottoman Empire grew more unified and stronger.

282. Napoleon's military venture in Egypt resulted in which discovery in an unrelated field?

(A) Gold deposits were found in the Nile Delta region by French sailors.

(B) New trade routes were opened to the Red Sea and Indian Ocean.

(C) The Rosetta Stone was found, which enabled translation of hieroglyphics.

(D) Egyptian-built steam engines were quickly adopted by France.

—Written description of the prophet Muhammad. Hilye by Kazasker
Mustafa Izzet Efendi (1801–1876).

283. The above image from the nineteenth century about the Muslim prophet
Muhammad represents a continuity in Sunni Islamic tradition in that

(A) It adheres to a mystical and less doctrinaire form of Islam
(B) It shows an image that borrows heavily from Buddhist influences
(C) It refrains from depicting any human image especially the prophet
(D) It uses phrases and words from both the Old and New Testaments

284. Which of the following changes were introduced into the Middle East in
the early 1800s and would later challenge the image above?

(A) Gunpowder weapons
(B) Printing press
(C) Radio technology
(D) Cameras

Hatt-ı Hümayun granted that all forms of religion freely worshiped, no subject hindered in the exercise of the religion, nor be in any way annoyed. No one shall be compelled to change their religion.

Hatt-ı Hümayun granted that all the subjects, without distinction, shall be received into the Civil and Military Schools. Every community is authorized to establish Public Schools of Science, Art, and Industry. However, in these public schools the methods of instruction and the choice of professors in schools of this class shall be under the control of a "Mixed Council of Public Instruction (Council of Public Instruction)" (Education ministry).

Hatt-ı Hümayun granted that there will be formulation of the new Codes; penal, correctional, and commercial laws, and rules of procedure and they were translated and published in all the languages

—Excerpt from the Tanzimat Reforms.

285. Which group in Ottoman society would be most upset by the changes described above?

(A) Turkish Muslims
(B) Armenian Christians
(C) Ottoman Jews
(D) Arab Muslims

286. The Tanzimat reforms represented which of the following changes in the Ottoman Empire?

(A) Imperialism
(B) Modernization
(C) Mechanization
(D) Nationalism

287. Which of the following historical events prompted the Ottomans to begin the Tanzimat reforms?

(A) Russo-Japanese war
(B) The Auspicious Event
(C) Battle of the Pyramids
(D) The Crimean War

FIGURES ON NATIONALITIES WITHIN THE OTTOMAN EMPIRE

Ethnic Group (Total Population) Percentage of Empire	Subgroup	Subgroup Population
Turkish group (14,020,000) 49.1%	Ottoman Turks Turkomans Tatars	13,500,000 300,000 220,000
Greco-Latin group (3,520,000) 12.3%	Greeks Kutzo-Vlachs Albanians	2,100,000 220,000 1,200,000
Slavic group (4,550,000) 15.9%	Serbo-Croatians Bulgarians Cossacks Lipovans	1,500,000 3,000,000 32,000 18,000
Georgian group (1,020,000) 3.6%	Circassians Lazes	1,000,000 20,000
Indian group (212,000) 0.7%	Gypsies	212,000
Persian group (3,620,000) 12.7%	Armenians Kurds Druze, Mutawalis, Nusayris, and Yazidis	2,500,000 1,000,000 120,000
Semites (1,611,000) 5.6%	Jews Arabs Syrian-Chaldaeans Maronites	158,000 1,000,000 160,000 293,000

Total Population of the Ottoman Empire, 1876: 28,553,000

288. The series of reforms around the mid-nineteenth century that put all Ottomans, regardless of religion or ethnicity, on an equal footing legally was called

(A) The 100 Days of Reform
(B) The Tanzimat Reforms
(C) The Meiji Reforms
(D) The Dhimmi Reforms

289. By the end of the nineteenth century, which of the following was a result of the Ottoman division of its subjects by ethnicity and region?

(A) A rise in nationalism among the empire's ethnicities

(B) Calls for the creation of a worker-led state

(C) A migration of peoples to the Americas from Eurasia

(D) The expansion of the Ottoman Empire in Asia

290. Initial expansion of Western-style university systems, communication methods, railways, and newspaper production and the promulgation of a European-style constitution are associated with which period in the history of the Ottoman Empire?

(A) World War I era

(B) Era of Suleyman the Magnificent

(C) Great Depression era

(D) Tanzimat reform era

291. The nineteenth-century Egyptian political leader Muhammad Ali is best known for

(A) Revitalization of Islamic fundamentalism in the Ottoman world

(B) Defeat of the British navy to prevent Greek independence

(C) Determined but ultimately unsuccessful efforts to modernize Egypt's economy along Western lines

(D) Breaking Egyptian dependence on cotton exports in trade relations

292. Which of the following made Egypt an attractive target for Western imperialist expansion in the late nineteenth century?

(A) Gold deposits

(B) Control of Nile River trade

(C) Lucrative tourism prospects

(D) Construction and control of the Suez Canal

293. Which statement best characterizes Ottoman and Qing Chinese relations with the West by about 1750?

(A) Both empires were in full military retreat and subject to carrying out Western economic demands.

(B) Both empires were successfully carrying out policies of isolation from the West.

(C) Qing China was able to strongly regulate relations with the West while Ottoman rulers were less able to repel Western incursions into their territorial waters.

(D) Qing China pursued a policy of imitation of Western industrial and mercantile practices while Ottoman rulers refused to do so.

"SAVE ME FROM MY FRIENDS!"

—Political cartoon depicting the Afghan Emir Sher Ali with his "friends" the Russian Bear and British Lion (1878).

294. The cartoon above is best understood in the context of which of the following?

(A) Hundred Days of Reform in Western China

(B) Janissary revolt or Auspicious Incident

(C) Power rivalries or "Great Game" in Central Asia

(D) Sunni and Shitte divide over the caliphate

295. Which of the following mirrors the situation that the peoples of Central Asia found themselves in dealing with outside powers?

(A) Scramble for Africa

(B) Sepoy Rebellion

(C) Treaty of Kanagawa

(D) Suez Crisis

—Robert Clive and Mir Jafar after the Battle of Plassey, 1757.

296. In the painting above, which of the following changes in Indian political life occurs?

(A) Elephants are now being traded by the British to China and Southeast Asia.

(B) The East India Company rises to become a major power on the subcontinent.

(C) The Islamic empires like the Mughals now start using gunpowder weapons.

(D) The Dutch and Portuguese go to war over control over Sri Lanka.

297. Which rival European power did the British defeat in the eighteenth century in its drive to control the Indian subcontinent?

(A) Netherlands

(B) France

(C) Italy

(D) Portugal

We desire no extension of our present territorial possessions; and, while we will permit no aggression upon our dominions or our rights to be attempted with impunity, we shall sanction no encroachment on those of others. We shall respect the rights, dignity, and honor of native princes as our own and we desire that they, as well as our own subjects, should enjoy that prosperity and that social advancement which can only be secured by internal peace and by good government. . . .

Firmly relying ourselves on the truth of Christianity, and acknowledging with gratitude ;the solace of religion, we disclaim alike the right and the desire to impose our convictions on any of our subjects. We declare it to be our royal will and pleasure that none be in anywise favored, none molested or disquieted, by reason of their religious faith or observances, but that all shall alike enjoy the equal and impartial protection of the law. . . .

Our clemency will be extended to all offenders, save and except those who have been or shall be convicted of having directly taken part in the murder of British subjects. With regard to such, the demands of justice forbid mercy. To all others in arms against the government we hereby promise unconditional pardon, amnesty, . . . of all offenses against ourselves, our crown and dignity, on the return to their homes and peaceful pursuits.

> —Queen Victoria. In 1858. Victoria proclaims the principles
> by which India will henceforth be ruled. Edited excerpt.

298. Which of the following continuity can be seen in Queen Victoria's proclamation in 1858?
    (A) The British self-confidence on the superiority of the Christian religion
    (B) The British desire to not extend their present territorial possessions
    (C) The British respect for the rights of the native princes or maharajahs
    (D) The British level of control over the Indian economy and taxation

299. What would provide context on why Queen Victoria sought to include the phrase "We declare it to be our royal will and pleasure that none be in anywise favored, none molested or disquieted, by reason of their religious faith or observances" in her proclamation?
    (A) It was hoped that many Indians would convert to Christianity.
    (B) Victoria is knowledgeable that Muslims were the majority of the Indian population.
    (C) It was a lack of religious sensibilities that caused the Sepoy Rebellion.
    (D) The East India Company was not interested in promoting the Hindu religion.

One industrial initiative in India developed around Calcutta, where British colonial rule had centered since the East India Company founded the city in 1690. A Hindu Brahman family, the Tagores, established close ties with many British administrators. Without becoming British, they sponsored a number of efforts to revivify India, including new colleges and research centers. Dwarkanath Tagore controlled tax collection in part of Bengal, and early in the 19th century he used part of his profit to found a bank. He also bought up a variety of commercial landholdings and traditional manufacturing operations. In 1834 he joined with British capitalists to establish a diversified company that boasted holdings in mines (including the first Indian coal mine), sugar refineries, and some new textile factories; the equipment was imported from Britain. Tagore's dominant idea was a British-Indian economic and cultural collaboration that would revitalize his country. He enjoyed a high reputation in Europe and for a short time made a success of his economic initiatives. Tagore died on a trip abroad, and his financial empire declined soon after. This first taste of Indian industrialization was significant, but it brought few immediate results. The big news in India, even as Tagore launched his companies, was the rapid decline of traditional textiles under the bombardment of British factory competition; millions of Indian villagers were thrown out of work. Furthermore, relations between Britain and the Indian elite worsened after the mid-1830s as British officials sought a more active economic role and became more intolerant of Indian culture. One British official, admitting no knowledge of Indian scholarship, wrote that "all the historical information" and science available in Sanskrit was "less valuable than what may be found in the most paltry abridgements used at preparatory schools in England." With these attitudes, the kind of collaboration that might have aided Indian appropriation of British industry became impossible.

Source: Peter Stearns, historian,
The Industrial Revolution in World History, 1993.

300. The British view of Indian culture discussed in the passage is best understood in the context of which of the following?

(A) Changes in Indian government as a result of the Enlightenment

(B) Emerging racial ideologies that were used to justify imperialism

(C) The rise of Marxist ideas regarding the working class

(D) The migration of Indian laborers overseas for plantation labor

301. Which of the following was an effect of the decline in Indian industries discussed in the passage?

(A) India's economy became dependent on Britain for natural resources and raw materials.

(B) India's participation in the world economy declined significantly.

(C) India's economy shifted from producing manufactured goods like cotton textiles to exporting raw materials like cotton.

(D) India's economy relied on the import of British food supplies and culinary expertise.

To sum up the whole, the British rule has been: morally, a great blessing; politically, peace and order on one hand, blunders on the other; materially, impoverishment, relieved as far as the railway and other loans go. The natives call the British system "Sakar ki Churi," the knife of sugar. That is to say, there is no oppression, it is all smooth and sweet, but it is the knife, notwithstanding. I mention this that you should know these feelings. Our great misfortune is that you do not know our wants. When you will know our real wishes, I have not the least doubt that you would do justice. The genius and spirit of the British people is fair play and justice.

—Dadabhai Naoroji in a speech to a London audience in 1871.

302. A historian studying the Raj period of India would find this account most useful for understanding the views of which group of Indians towards British rule?
    (A) Hindu Peasants
    (B) Muslim Merchants
    (C) Colonial elites
    (D) British civil servants

303. Which of the following is generally true of indigenous individuals promoted to assist Western imperialists in their rule of the colony?
    (A) When possible, Christians were chosen.
    (B) They tended to be from minority ethnic groups.
    (C) They were given limited Western education and technical training.
    (D) All of the above.

—Magazine sketch called Christmas in India, in *The Graphic*, 1881.

304. Which of the following changes in migration patterns for the British in India is reflected in the image above?

(A) Family units were becoming more common among British settlers.

(B) British settlers brought their family servants with them to India.

(C) British settlers practiced polygamy to assimilate to Muslim India.

(D) British settlers were now being housed in tents rather than houses.

305. Which of the following acts as a major cause for the scene in the British newspaper, The Graphic, in 1881?

(A) The use of Indian servants by expatriate families

(B) The use of sepoy troops in British armed forces

(C) Improved transportation and health services

(D) An increase in available food for British settlers

306. Which of the following was NOT a reason India had become Britain's most important colony by about 1800?

(A) India offered crucial port facilities for the British navy.

(B) India was a major outlet for British manufactured goods.

(C) India was an important supplier of British raw materials.

(D) India was an important location for British textile factories.

307. During the era of British colonialism in India, why were the British content, in general, to leave Indian social hierarchies intact?

    (A) Over time, exposure to Hindu doctrine on caste won British elites over.

    (B) British officials were able to, in essence, graft themselves onto an existing social pyramid at its apex while incurring a minimum of social disruption.

    (C) British notions of proper gender roles, such as a wife's duty to commit sati, were the same as Indian ones.

    (D) Superior Mughal political and military authority prevented British interference in Indian social relations.

308. Which reform was most emblematic of growing British interest in transforming Indian social relations in the nineteenth century?

    (A) Dismantling of the caste system

    (B) Prohibition of sati

    (C) Expansion of education for girls

    (D) Building interest in the sport of cricket

309. By what method did Western imperialists work to gain a dependable corps of local managers to aid in the administration of their colonies?

    I. Kidnapping of regents' family members and holding them for ransom

    II. Conversion of local elites to Christianity

    III. Education of new generations of colonized youth in Western languages and cultural practices

    (A) I and II

    (B) II and III

    (C) I and III

    (D) II only

310. Founded in 1885, the India Congress Party's early membership like M. K. Gandhi, consisted largely of which group?

    (A) Middle-class professionals

    (B) Working-class men only

    (C) Rajputs and maharajahs

    (D) Landed peasants

SLAVERS REVENGING THEIR LOSSES.

—Newspaper sketch from the nineteenth century.

311. The image above depicts non-Europeans enslaving Africans and bringing them to European slavers. Which of the following best explains why Europeans did NOT conduct such slave raids themselves?

(A) Wild African animals
(B) Deadly African diseases
(C) Difficult African terrain
(D) Monsoon trade winds

312. The image above is often referred to as which of the following terms?

(A) *The Middle Passage*
(B) *The Gold-Salt trade*
(C) *Journey to the Coast*
(D) *The Spice Route*

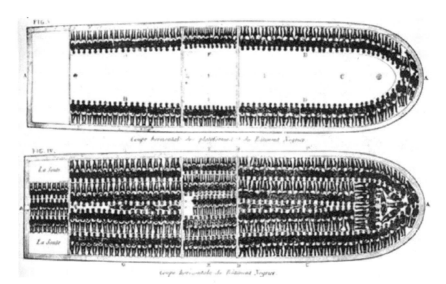

—Diagram of a slave ship from the Atlantic slave trade. From evidence delivered before the British House of Commons in 1790 and 1791.

313. The image above, which gave a glimpse into the horrors of the Atlantic Slave trade, helped popularize which social movement?

(A) suffrage
(B) Right to unionize
(C) Religious tolerance
(D) Abolition

314. The image above helped bring about which important change in world history?

(A) The ban on torture in the British act system
(B) The end of slavery in the Atlantic world
(C) The refitting of ocean going passenger ships
(D) The addition of lifeboats in case of storms

We have the power in our hands, moral, physical, and mechanical; the first, based on the Bible; the second, upon the wonderful adaptation of the Anglo-Saxon race to all climates, situations, and circumstances . . . the third, bequeathed [given] to us by the immortal James Watt. By his invention [of the steam engine] every river is laid open to us, time and distance are shortened. If his spirit is allowed to witness the success of his invention here on earth, I can conceive no application of it that would meet his approbation [approval] more than seeing the mighty streams of the Mississippi and the Amazon, the Niger and the Nile, the Indus and the Ganges, stemmed by hundreds of steam-vessels, carrying the glad tidings of "peace and good will towards men" into the dark places of the earth which are now filled with cruelty. This power, which has only been in existence for a quarter of a century, has rendered rivers truly "the highway of nations," and made easy what it would have been difficult if not impossible, to accomplish without it. . . .

—Macgregor Laird, Scottish explorer and shipbuilder,
wrote this narrative after travelling by steamship up the
Niger River in West Africa between 1832 and 1834.

315. Which of the following best explains the historical circumstances that led to British exploration in West Africa in the 1830s?
    (A) British Industrial power
    (B) British moral superiority
    (C) British desire for tea
    (D) British limited monarchy

316. Which of the following best describes his attitudes toward European and non-Western cultures?
    (A) Socialist
    (B) Social Darwinist
    (C) Misogynist
    (D) Indifference

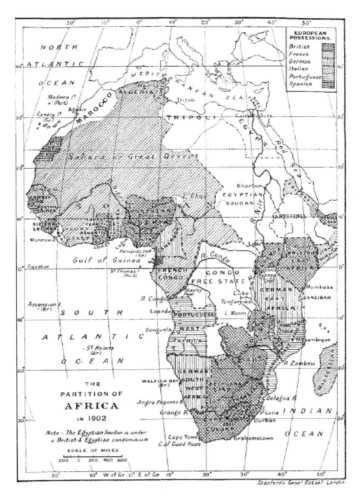

—Map of African showing political divisions.

317. Many of the political divisions shown on this map were directly related to the

(A) Slave trade
(B) Boer War
(C) Opium Wars
(D) Berlin Conference

318. The political divisions in Africa were based primarily on which of the following factors?

(A) Geographic and topographic features
(B) Linguistic and cultural differences
(C) European desires and claims
(D) The location of manufacturing centers

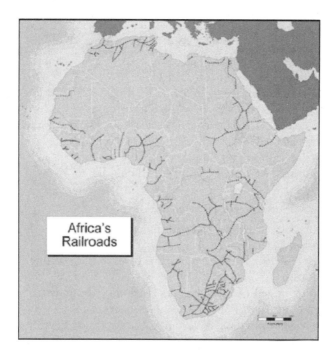

319. Based on the image above of Africa during the late nineteenth century and early twentieth century, one effect of European imperialism on Africa was

(A) The improvement of working conditions in Africa
(B) That African economies became dependent on the exportation of raw materials
(C) Africans' acceptance of the doctrine of the "White Man's Burden"
(D) Widespread Western education and literacy of African peoples

320. Many of the nations colonized were rich in natural resources. How did Social Darwinists view the mining of natural resources in these colonized lands?

(A) It was their right to take what they wanted.
(B) It was a necessity for their colonies to survive.
(C) It was a way to preserve traditional economies.
(D) It was a way to protect Africans from the Industrial Revolution.

321. Which of the following best describes the impact of slavery on African demographics from the eighteenth to the twentieth century?

(A) The eastern shores of Africa were mostly affected.
(B) The demographic loss was offset by population growth.
(C) It was the interior of Africa that most felt its impact.
(D) It primarily affected the societies of North Africa.

322. Which of the following best characterizes the difference between educational systems set up by imperialists in Africa and India?

(A) African colonies contained comparatively more schools administered by colonial governments than India.

(B) African schools tended to be set up by Christian missionaries while Indian ones were set up by the colonial state.

(C) Indian education mainly consisted of trade schools for training industrial workers, while African schools did not.

(D) African education mainly consisted of trade schools for training industrial workers, while Indian schools did not.

323. The purpose of the Berlin Conference of 1885 was

(A) For representatives of Western industry to learn cutting-edge German industrial techniques

(B) For representatives of colonized peoples to learn cutting-edge German industrial techniques

(C) To set quotas and agreements surrounding the growth of the German navy

(D) To negotiate settlements among Western rivalries over the partition of Africa

324. Which thinker is most closely associated with formulating the theories of "Social Darwinism"?

(A) Karl Marx

(B) Jean-Jacques Rousseau

(C) Thomas Hobbes

(D) Herbert Spencer

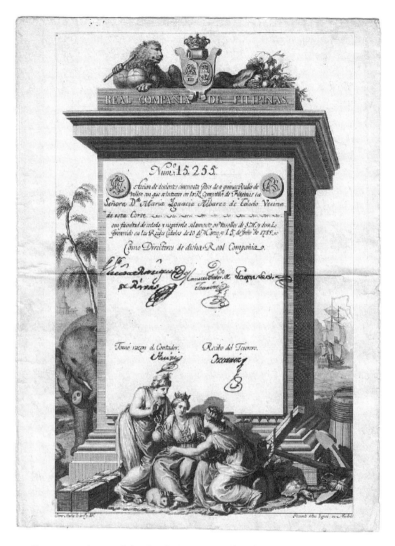

—Corporate share of the Real Compañia de Filipinas (Royal Philippine Company), which had a monopoly on trade in the Americas for Spanish monarchy, issued 1785.

325. Which economic system determined the regulations that governed the Royal Philippine Company in the Spanish empire?

(A) European mercantilist laws

(B) Laissez-faire principles

(C) Renaissance guild by-laws

(D) Medieval manorialism

326. The rules regulating the joint-stock companies, like the Royal Philippine Company, gave them a monopoly on colonial trade and colonial critics claimed that they impeded local businesses. Which of the following regions were also upset at the economic rules that governed the use of monopoly over colonial trade?

(A) The Low countries
(B) Russian empire
(C) American colonies
(D) Siberian steppe

By the late eighteenth century the French colony at San-Domingue had become the largest producer of arguably the New World's most important commodity—sugar. Loss of this colony to the "excesses" of liberty" that the French Revolution had inspired among the enslaved population on that island was intolerable to the ruling classes that emerged in France by the turn of the nineteenth century. In May 1802, Napoleon's force tried to reestablish slavery in Haiti. Toussaint L'Ouverture, leader of the Haitian Revolution, was kidnapped and deported back to France. The effect was to enrage the black majority and provoke even greater rebellion. By now black soldiers had gained experience in organizing an army. The French were at a disadvantage, they were more susceptible to disease (particularly yellow fever) than their opponents and reinforcements were difficult to obtain from France. The French troops were also demoralized by fighting against enemies who sang La Marseillaise and invoked revolutionary ideas. One officer, Lacroix, asked, "Have our barbarous enemies justice on their side? Are we no longer the soldiers of Republican France? And have we become the crude instruments of Policy.

—Mark Almond, historian

327. The secondary source above supports which of the following conclusions?
   (A) French soldiers sent to Haiti had more immunity to disease than Haitians fighting for their homeland.
   (B) Napoleon's soldiers sent Toussaint L'Ouverture back to Haiti where he died of yellow fever.
   (C) British and French soldiers fought together to end slavery in the Americas as a whole.
   (D) Some French soldiers in Haiti questioned the incompatibility of their mission with Republican values.

328. Which factor had the LEAST impact on creating the conditions that gave rise to the situation described in the passage?
   (A) The French island colony of Haiti was extremely valuable for France because of its sugar crop.
   (B) Slavery was first established in Santo Domingue/Haiti in the early 1700s by French traders and settlers.
   (C) French revolutionary ideas such as equality and democracy began to spread to Haiti by 1790.
   (D) The British anti-slavery movement was established by the Quaker and Evangelical Christian community.

Military Rule in Latin America to 1900

Country	Date of Independence	Periods of Military Rule	Total Years of Military Rule
Columbia	1831		0
El Salvador	1830		0
Costa Rica	1830		0
Nicaragua	1830	1855–1857	2
Brazil	1821	1889–1894	5
Uruguay	1830	1876–1886	10
Honduras	1830	1830–1847	17
Peru	1825	1846–1854 1884–1895	19
Ecuador	1830	1851–1856 1861–1875 1878–1882 1892–1895	28
Guatemala	1830	1840–1865 1871–1885	39
Bolivia	1825	1848–1870 1876–1880	26
Chile	1818	1818–1851	33
Haiti	1804	1804–1843 1847–1859	47
Venezuela	1830	1831–1835 1839–1843 1846–1858 1861–1868	49
Paraguay	1815	1815–1869 1894–1898	57
Mexico	1821	1823–1843 1846–1855 1863–1867	33

329. Which of the following acts as context for the chart on the left?

(A) The lack of economic development in Latin America

(B) The political instability in many Latin American nations

(C) The political dominance of the Catholic church

(D) The migration of French revolutionaries to the Americas

330. Causation for the political process in the chart on the left is due to which of the following?

(A) Enlightenment writings and ideas

(B) The abolition of slavery

(C) The Industrial Revolution

(D) Sharp racial and class divisions

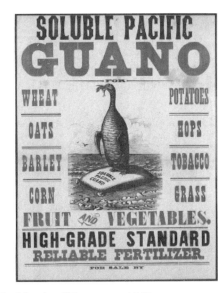

—Photograph of guano mining in the Islands off Peru, circa 1860.

—Advertisement for guano, which is bird droppings and found on islands off South America.

331. Which of the following least explains causation for the use of almost exclusively Chinese labor in the guano fields of the islands off Peru?

(A) The ending of the slave trade of Africans
(B) Overpopulation in China during the nineteenth century
(C) The attitude of the Qing that such laborers were disloyal
(D) Improved methods of transportation and communication

332. The sale of guano fertilizer by nations like Peru and Chile shows a strong continuity in the period before and after political independence, in terms of which of the following?

(A) The export of American raw materials to wealthier nations
(B) The import of Chinese to make up for labor shortages
(C) The use of advertisements to reach a new and larger market
(D) The influence of European revolutionary ideas

333. The combination of a cheap raw material, a labor force that is mobile, advertising and transportation to wealthy markets indicate which fact about the world's economy by the 1900?

(A) Interdependence
(B) Importation
(C) Disconnection
(D) Socialism

—Photograph of Mexico City, 1890.

334. Which examples of modernity from the Porfirio Diaz regime in Mexico can be seen in the photograph?

(A) Market stalls
(B) Electrical lines
(C) Horse and carriages
(D) Tree-lined streets

335. The image above shows a street in Mexico City in 1890 as an example of the success of the Porfirio Diaz regime. Which of the following was NOT an aspect of the regime?

(A) Foreign investment
(B) Crony capitalism
(C) Persistent poverty
(D) Democratic rights

336. Which of the following concerns made Creole elites, who yearned for independence from Spain, what we might call "cautious revolutionaries"?

(A) Fear that the Spanish monarchs were more capable rulers
(B) Fear that continued rapid industrialization would create urban instability
(C) A growing communist threat inspired by the example of the Bolshevik Revolution in the Soviet Union
(D) Fear that slaves and other oppressed groups would target local elites as part of a general social upheaval

337. Which is the best reason why rail networks were underdeveloped in Spanish Latin America at the time independence was achieved?

    (A) Colonial-era Latin American mining was not profitable enough to warrant rail investment.

    (B) No cash crops were produced for export.

    (C) Rail technology was relatively new and limited to small areas of Britain, Western Europe, and the United States at the time.

    (D) Latin American mountains and rivers made rail construction impossible.

338. What impact did the instability of the wars for independence have on subsequent developments in Latin America?

    (A) Agricultural regions devastated by modern warfare were slow to recover, leading to widespread famine.

    (B) Female veterans of military service refused subordinate roles in the home.

    (C) Military leaders remained influential and intervened frequently in political affairs.

    (D) Mestizo, slave, and indigenous populations formed guerrilla units and launched armed struggle for communism.

339. Which Latin American nation attracted the greatest number of European immigrants in the late nineteenth and early twentieth centuries?

    (A) Colombia

    (B) Peru

    (C) Venezuela

    (D) Argentina

340. Which situation did formally independent Latin American nations have most in common with colonized portions of Africa and Asia in the nineteenth century?

    (A) Rapidly expanding social, economic, and political possibilities for the majority of women

    (B) A dependent position in the world economy due to the rise of Western industrial capitalism

    (C) Declining importance of race and ethnicity in defining social status

    (D) Supplantation of agriculture by industry as the main occupation of the laboring population

Population of the Hawaiian Islands In the Pacific, 1778–1878

Year	Population
1778	242,000
1823	135,000
1831–32	124,000
1835–36	107,000
1850	84,000
1853*	73,000
1860	70,000
1866	63,000
1872	57,000
1878**	58,000

*97.5% of the population born in Hawaii

**83.6% of the population born in Hawaii

341. Which of the following explains the changes in the Hawaiian population?

   (A) Gunpowder weapons such as breech-loading rifles
   (B) Deadly hurricanes, tsunamis, and volcanoes
   (C) Disease-related deaths due to lack of Hawaiian's immunity
   (D) Changes in Hawaiian marriage customs and birth control

342. Which of the following was a similarity that Hawaii shared with the people of the Americas, Siberia, Australia, and other indigenous peoples in their interaction with Europeans?

   (A) Conversion to Roman Catholic Christianity
   (B) Long-standing geographic isolation
   (C) Adoption of the English language
   (D) Acceptance of Dutch learning

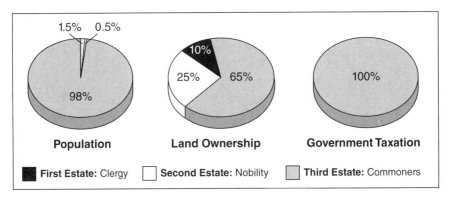

Source: Jackson J. Spielvogel, *World History*, Glencoe/McGraw-Hill, 2003 (adapted)

343. The pie charts above are best understood in the context of
(A) Conditions that led to the French Revolution
(B) European practice of slavery in France
(C) Industrial Revolution effects on workers
(D) Patriarchy in pre-Revolutionary France

344. As seen in the pie charts above question 343, compared to the American Revolution, the French Revolution
(A) Had less impact on the world's supply of cotton and tobacco
(B) Was also brought about by the poor conditions of the bourgeoisie
(C) Was a social upheaval as well as a political revolution
(D) Led to the rise of a military general who ruled as dictator

This great increase in the quantity of work, which, in consequence of the division of labour, the same number of people are capable of performing, is owing to three different circumstances; first, to the increase of dexterity in every particular workman; secondly, to the saving of the time which is commonly lost in passing from one species of work to another; and, lastly, to the invention of a great number of machines which facilitate and abridge labor, and enable one man to do the work of many.

—Adam Smith, *The Wealth of Nations*, 1776.

345. According to Adam Smith in his seminal work, *The Wealth of Nations*, 1776, which of the following is true?

   (A) The division of labor leads to greater output of production.
   (B) The dexterity of workers increased through industrialization.
   (C) Productivity of machines decreased due to lack of resources.
   (D) The world's population decreased because of mechanization.

346. The principle outlined above by Adam Smith was key to the success of which historical process?

   (A) Western Imperialism
   (B) Industrial Revolution
   (C) Scientific Revolution
   (D) Growth of Democracy

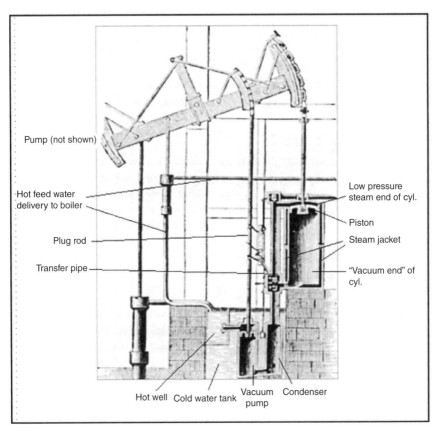

—Schematic design of James Watt's steam engine, patented in 1750

347. The image left showing James Watt's steam engine patent in 1750 that was a result of which of the following historical events and processes?

(A) The practical application of science in technology

(B) The Enlightenment thought on natural rights

(C) The development of iron and bronze technology

(D) The Colombian Exchange of plants and animals

348. All of the following are historical factors that help explain Britain's role as a leader of industrialization EXCEPT:

(A) the government's support of patents that protected innovation

(B) the rich deposits of iron and coal lying close together in the British Isles

(C) the lack of an educated middle class with an entrepreneurial attitude

(D) the building of transportation infrastructure

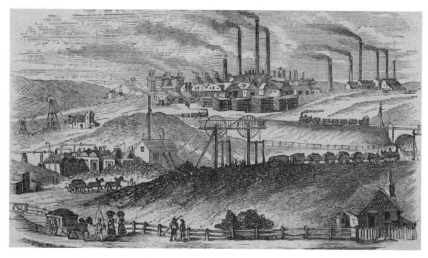

—Print showing a nineteenth-century factory in the British Midlands.

349. The image above is best explained by which of the following processes during the Industrial Revolution?

(A) Domestic System to Factory System

(B) Rural population to urban populations

(C) Luddite activity to Union creation

(D) Market Revolution to Russian Revolution

350. What other mid-eighteenth and early nineteenth-century development came alongside improvements in productivity?

(A) Urban poverty became less visible and declined.

(B) The social standing of working women to men was equal.

(C) The growth of existing large cities expanded rapidly.

(D) Sanitation and availability of fresh water improved.

"Heaven helps those who help themselves" is a well-tried maxim, embodying in a small compass the results of vast human experience. The spirit of self-help is the root of all genuine growth in the individual; and, exhibited in the lives of many, it constitutes the true source of national vigor and strength. Help from without is often enfeebling in its effects, but help from within invariably invigorates. Whatever is done for men or classes, to a certain extent takes away the stimulus and necessity of doing for themselves; and where men are subjected to over-guidance and over-government, the inevitable tendency is to render them comparatively helpless. Even the best institutions can give a man no active help. Perhaps the most they can do is, to leave him free to develop himself and improve his individual condition. But in all times men have been prone to believe that their happiness and well-being were to be secured by means of institutions rather than by their own conduct. Hence the value of legislation as an agent in human advancement has usually been much over-estimated.

—Samuel Smiles, Scottish author, in *Self-Help*, 1859.

351. Smiles' argument is best understood in the context of which of the following?
    (A) Discontent among the owners of transnational business over trade regulation
    (B) Disputes among factory workers over wages and working hours
    (C) Conflicting visions of Marxists and union members in addressing working conditions
    (D) Debates over the role of government in implementing social and urban reforms

352. Smiles' view regarding legislation would most likely be supported by which of the following groups?
    (A) Factory workers
    (B) Marxist socialists
    (C) *Laissez-faire* capitalists
    (D) The merchant class

—Newspaper drawing of Luddittes smashing a power loom in 1812

353. The Luddite movement of early nineteenth-century England is best seen as

   (A) A reaction to the Industrial Revolution
   (B) A reaction to Communist ideology
   (C) Supporters of Social Darwinism
   (D) A reaction to population increases

354. How did Karl Marx suggest the workers ought to resolve their conflict with their employers?

   (A) Return to life as a rural peasant and take up subsistence farming similar to life before industrialization
   (B) Continue his efforts to smash the machines and return the economy to the era of small-scale handicraft production
   (C) Take up arms, establish rule of the proletariat and institute public ownership of the means of production
   (D) Cooperate with industrial capitalists to boost efficiency and output for the benefit of the state

In spite of the fact that we have no such fleet as we should have, we have con-quered for ourselves a place in the sun. It will now be my task to see to it that this place in the sun shall remain our undisputed possession, in order that the sun's rays may fall fruitfully upon our activity and trade in foreign parts, that our industry and agriculture may develop within the state and our sailing sports upon the water, for our future lies upon the water. The more Germans go out upon the waters, whether it be in races or regattas, whether it be in journeys across the ocean, or in the service of the battle flag, so much the better it will be for us. . . . As head of the Empire I therefore rejoice over every citizen, whether from Hamburg, Bremen, or Lübeck, who goes forth with this large outlook and seeks new points where we can drive in the nail on which to hang our armor. . . .

—Kaiser Wilhelm II of Germany in a speech to the North German
Regatta Association, 1901.

355. The speech by Wilhelm II best illustrates which of the following patterns of the period, 1750–1900?

(A) The growing demand for settler colonists to alleviate population pressures

(B) The establishment of transoceanic empires by industrial powers

(C) The rise of resistance movements opposing imperialism

(D) The use of religious ideologies to justify the imperial expansion

356. The speech by the German Kaiser Wilhelm II aligns most strongly with which of the following beliefs?

(A) Social Darwinism

(B) Marxism

(C) Appeasement

(D) Industrialization

357. Which of the following was a new Western motive for overseas territorial expansion in the industrial era?

(A) Missionary drive to convert non-Western peoples to Christianity

(B) Seizure of land to be put to use raising cash crops

(C) Drive to dominate sources of precious minerals and metals

(D) Need for raw materials for factory production

358. Which answer choice best captures the changes historians associate with what is termed the "second industrial revolution"?

(A) Industrialization outside of England
(B) Shift to nuclear power in the West after World War II
(C) Central role of heavy industry and electrical power
(D) Rapid urbanization associated with factory production

359. Which choice lays out the correct order in which the Industrial Revolution began and spread?

(A) Great Britain, United States, continental Europe
(B) Continental Europe, United States, Great Britain,
(C) United States, continental Europe, Great Britain
(D) Great Britain, continental Europe, United States

360. Which of the Western societies expanded democratic rights in the first half of the nineteenth century but did not experience the mass upheavals of 1848?

   I. Great Britain
  II. France
 III. The United States

(A) I and II
(B) II and III
(C) I and III
(D) I, II, and III

361. Which of the following causes did the American and French Revolutions share?

   I. Frustration over high levels of taxation
  II. Resentment at exclusion from governmental decision making
 III. Anger sparked by feudal exploitation of the peasantry

(A) I and II
(B) II and III
(C) I and III
(D) I only

*A few steps from the road I noticed a peasant who was ploughing his field. . . .
It was Sunday then. . . . The peasant was ploughing with great care. "Have
you not any time to work during the week, that you work on a Sunday, and
at that in a great heat?" "In the week, sir, there are six days, and we have to
work for the manor six times a week, and in the evening we haul the hay
from the meadows, if the weather is good; and on holidays the women and
girls go to the woods to gather mushrooms and berries. . . ." Do you work the
same way for your master? "No, sir! It would be sinful to work the same way;
he has in his fields one hundred hands for one mouth, and I have but two
hands for seven mouths, if you count it up. If you were to work yourself to
death at your master's work, he would not thank you for it. The master will
not pay the capitation tax; he will let you have no mutton, no hempen cloth,
no chicken, no butter. . . . The conversation with this agriculturist awak-
ened a multitude of thoughts in me. Above all, I thought of the inequality
of the peasant's condition. I compared the crown peasants with those of the
proprietors. Both live in villages, but while the first pay a stated tax, the others have to be ready to pay whatever the master wishes. The first are judged
by their peers; the others are dead to the laws, except in criminal matters. A
member of society only then is taken cognizance of by the Government that
protects him when he violates the social bond, when he becomes a criminal!
That thought made all my blood boil. Beware, cruel proprietor! On the brow
of every one of your peasants I see your condemnation! . . ."*

—From the *Journey from St. Petersburg to Moscow* of
Alexander Nikolaevich Radishchev, 1790.

362. Which of the following provides context for the historical situation
described in the reading?

(A) Russian autocracy
(B) Russian serfdom
(C) Russian semi-isolation
(D) Russian transportation

363. Which of the following can be argued is a result of the continuation of
serfdom in Russian till the mid-nineteenth century?

(A) Russia's late development of a modern economy
(B) Russia's vast size and large population
(C) Russia's Eastern Orthodox Christian religion
(D) Russia's practice of slavery and indentured servitude

Development of the Extractive Industries

Product	1877	1887	1892	1897
Coal	110	227	424	684
Oil	13	167	299	478
Cast iron	23	36	64	113
Iron	16	22	29	30
Steel	3	14	31	74

Russian in Comparison

Nation circa 1898	Coal in puds per Inhabitant	Cotton Lbs per Inhabitant
Britain	311	53
Germany	143	14
Belgium	204	NA
France	20	11
USA	162	28
Russia	5.8	5

Note: The term "puds" were a measurement at the time in iron and steel manufacturing.

364. Based on the first chart, which terms best fits the items Russia was recording for its industrialization program?

(A) Mercantile goods
(B) Agricultural goods
(C) Luxury items
(D) Industrial goods

365. Which of the following is the best conclusion of the two charts above?

(A) Russia was increasing production internally and overtaking its fellow European nations.
(B) While Russia had increased production internally, it lagged far behind other European nations.
(C) Russia was lagging behind in both domestic production as well as far behind other European states.
(D) Russian industrial output saw no change despite undertaking a program of industrialization.

—Cartoon from the American magazine, *Judge*, that shows US President Roosevelt saying to the Russian Czar, "Stop your cruel oppression of the Jews!"

366. What name was given to late nineteenth-century czarist policies that imposed Russian cultural values across the empire?

(A) Czarification
(B) Slavification
(C) Muscovication
(D) Russification

367. The oppression of Jews in the Russian empire later led to which of the following historical processes?

(A) The formation of guerilla bands to resist Czarist police and military
(B) The migration of millions of Jews to the Western Europe and the Americas
(C) The conversion of most Jews to Eastern Orthodox Christianity
(D) The sale of personal items to fund a tribute to the Russian state

368. Which pair of regional powers was able by 1900, to initiate substantial industrialization and resist Western domination?

(A) Ottoman Empire and South Africa
(B) Russia and Japan
(C) South Africa and Russia
(D) Argentina and Ottoman Empire

369. All of the following statements are reasons monarchy survived so much longer in Russia than it did anywhere else in Europe EXCEPT:

(A) The defeat of Napoleon in 1812 seemed to indicate a royal power could defeat a modern one
(B) Serfdom continued to provide a stable labor system
(C) Czars were able to mobilize enough industrial development to remain a world power
(D) The Romanov dynasty imitated the stable British model of constitutional monarchy

370. Which of the following decisions by Russian czars was motivated by a long-held desire for a warm-water port and access to trade of the Mediterrranean Sea?

(A) Construction of the trans-Siberian railway
(B) Launching the Crimean War
(C) Construction of St. Petersburg
(D) Annexation of Poland

Learn, O Lisbon, that the destroyers of our houses, palaces, churches, and con-
vents, the cause of the death of so many people and of the flames that devoured
such vast treasures, are your abominable sins, and not comets, stars, vapours and
exhalations, and similar natural phenomena. . . . It is scandalous to pretend the
earthquake was just a natural event, for if that be true, there is no need to repent
and to try to avert the wrath of God, and not even the Devil himself could
invent a false idea more likely to lead us all to irreparable ruin. Holy people had
prophesied the earthquake was coming, yet the city continued in its sinful ways
without a care for the future. Now, indeed, the case of Lisbon is desperate. It is
necessary to devote all our strength and purpose to the task of repentance. . . .

—Jesuit Priest Gabriel Malagrida,
"An Opinion on the True Cause of the Earthquake," 1756.

. . . even though earthquakes occur in this country fairly often and at all
seasons, the most terrible and most frequent ones are felt in the months of
autumn towards the end of the year. This observation is confirmed not only
by numerous cases in America, for apart from the destruction of the city of
Lima ten years ago, and that of another equally populous city in the previ-
ous century, very many examples have been noted, but also in our part of
the world we find, apart from the latest earthquake, many other historical
instances of earthquakes and volcanic eruptions that have occurred more fre-
quently in autumn than at any other time of the year.

—Immanuel Kant, German philosopher in one of three texts
attempting to explain the causes of earthquakes, 1756.

371. The first reading, the priest Malagrida blames which of the following for
the cause of the Lisbon earthquake of 1756?
(A) Climatic forces across the world
(B) Subterranean movements of lava
(C) The immorality of Lisbon's residents
(D) The recent apathy of Christian clergy

372. Emanuel Kant proposes that the causes of the earthquake were due to
(A) Seasonal changes
(B) Shifts in tectonic plates
(C) Human wickedness
(D) Monsoon winds

373. The triple tragedy in Lisbon of a devastating earthquake, tsunami waves,
and rampaging fires later led to which of the following historical processes
that was essential to the modern world?
(A) A rise in Christian fundamentalism in the West
(B) Scientific reasoning for natural phenomena
(C) Trade routes that avoided earthquake zones
(D) Technology that could predict tsunamis and earthquakes

—Ceiling painting at the former headquarters of the British East India Company, 1778.

374. Which of the following best represents the context for the painting above?

(A) A sharp decrease in cultural diffusion

(B) The spread of Western technology such as printing

(C) An increase in global economic integration

(D) The introduction of slavery into the Asian landmass

375. Which of the following is an interpretation of the above image?

(A) A grateful Eastern Hemisphere offering up its bounty to Great Britain

(B) Asian peoples being enslaved by the nations of the Americas

(C) Mythical figures from the classical world worshiping Zeus

(D) Trade between animist deities and Christian saints

376. Which of the following famous incidents was the British East India Company NOT involved in?

(A) Boston Tea Party

(B) China's Opium Wars

(C) India's Sepoy Rebellion

(D) Congress of Vienna

CHAPTER 4

The Present Era: 1900–Present

Controlling Idea: An "Age of Extremes"

Numerous terms have been used to describe this era such as "The Dark Century" and "The Bloody Twentieth Century." Dr. Eric Hobsbawn called it the Age of Extremes, and this phrase is a useful way to begin to conceptualize the dizzying scope and pace of change we have seen in the years since the opening shots of the First World War in 1914. Where before we had wars now we have world wars. Where before we had powers now we have seen superpowers. The explosion of technological innovation and productive capacity we saw in the Industrial Revolution has been expanded upon in ways individuals alive in 1914 could scarcely dream of. Yet all too familiar, in point of fact ancient, patterns of poverty still define life for billions of people. It is, then, an "Age of Extremes" in wealth and poverty and an "Age of Extremes" for the biosphere where we have reached the situation in which man-made gases contribute to planetary climate change. As the millennium approached, the global tapestry we see is one of an ever more connected world or globalization. We see the acceleration of movements of ideas, trade goods, and people. While there have been major disruptions with globalization, we also saw a rise in the standard of living to unprecedented levels.

—Cartoon in *Puck*, an American magazine published in 1900 in the aftermath of the Boxer rebellion in China.

377. The illustration would be most useful to a historian studying which of the following?

(A) European responses to the weakness of non-European states
(B) Chinese Confucian views of economic imperialism
(C) Tactics used by imperial powers to conquer territories
(D) Advances in military technology as a result of industrialization

378. Which of the following was most directly a result of the events shown in the cartoon?

(A) 1905 Russo-Japanese War
(B) 1905 Russian Revolution
(C) 1899 Boer War
(D) World War II in 1939

—Female students participate in a demonstration as part of the May Fourth Movement, 1919.

379. A similarity between the May Fourth Movement of 1919 and the Tiananmen Square demonstrations in 1989 is the actions of which of the following groups in Chinese society?

(A) Peasants
(B) Workers
(C) Students
(D) Warlords

380. The direct reason for the upsurge in Nationalist feeling was which of the following historical events in 1919?

(A) The rise of fascism
(B) The Versailles treaty
(C) The Boxer Rebellion
(D) The Long March

381. Based on the image above, which of the following can be said about the protesters?

(A) Foot-binding was no longer being practiced by many urban elites.
(B) The English language was spoken by most rural women.
(C) China was transitioning to being a matriarchal society.
(D) Communism was discarded as a viable economic theory.

A revolution is not a dinner party. . . . A revolution is an insurrection, an act of violence by which one class overthrows another. A rural revolution is a revolution by which the peasantry overthrows the power of the feudal landlord class. Without using the greatest force, the peasants cannot possibly overthrow the deep-rooted authority of the landlords which has lasted for thousands of years. The rural areas need a mighty revolutionary upsurge, for it alone can rouse the people in their millions to become a powerful force. All the actions mentioned here which have been labeled as "going too far" flow from the power of the peasants, which has been called forth by the mighty revolutionary upsurge in the countryside. . . . In this period it was necessary to establish the absolute authority of the peasants. It was necessary to forbid malicious criticism of the peasant associations. It was necessary to overthrow the whole authority of the gentry, to strike them to the ground and keep them there. There is revolutionary significance in all the actions which were labeled as "going too far" in this period. To put it bluntly, it is necessary to create terror for a while in every rural area, or otherwise it would be impossible to suppress the activities of the counter-revolutionaries in the countryside or overthrow the authority of the gentry. Proper limits have to be exceeded in order to right a wrong, or else the wrong cannot be righted.

—Mao Tse-Tung's Hunan Peasant Movement Investigation, 1927.

382. Which of the following historical arguments correctly relates to the reading above?

(A) Mao believed in the ability of capitalist countries to reform themselves to stave off revolution.

(B) Mao wanted to liberate the merchants from the bottom of the Confucian social class structure-

(C) Mao theorized that the rural masses would bow to the demands of the bourgeoisie city dwellers.

(D) In focusing on the peasants' revolutionary potential, Mao deviated from classical Marxist theory.

383. The line "A revolution is not a dinner party" is a clear reference to

(A) Cosmopolitan lifestyles

(B) Political violence

(C) Agrarian innovations

(D) Ideological purity

Circa 1960–1976.

384. Based on the image above, which other nation also used similar artistic style depicting women and a similar feminist message in its state propaganda?

(A) Fascist Italy
(B) Soviet Union
(C) Weimar Germany
(D) Showa Japan

385. Which of the following conclusions is true about women's rights in Mao's China?

(A) Due to the problems associated with the Great Leap Forward, women had no more rights than under the Qing dynasty.
(B) Women were given full equality by the state and soon achieved many positions in government, including the premiership.
(C) Women were given full reproductive rights as men plus, with no limits on family size.
(D) Although gains were made by women, the reality never lived up to the state propaganda.

386. Which development prompted Chinese nationalists and communists to suspend civil war and form a shaky common cause?

(A) Death of Sun Yat-sen

(B) Japanese invasion of China

(C) Massive American investment to build up industrial sectors in Chinese urban centers

(D) Communist long march to sanctuary in nationalist base areas in northwest China

387. Mao's campaign to infuse industrial development into the national economy at the commune level was called

(A) The Great Leap Forward

(B) New Democracy

(C) Protracted Warfare

(D) "Hundred Flowers" Period

388. The "Great Revolution for a Proletarian Culture" in China is best described as

(A) A massive Deng Xiaoping–era program for technical training of peasants in industrial techniques

(B) The strategic retreat during the 1930s led by Mao Zedong from southern China to base areas to the north and west

(C) A 1960s–era campaign where mass mobilizations of youth were employed to target and repress "capitalist roaders" in positions of authority and continue the violent revolutionary struggle for a communist society

(D) Student demonstrations for political reform in 1989 brutally suppressed by Chinese authorities

389. Which of the following best characterizes developments in China since 1979?

   I. Massive internal migration

  II. Strong export-driven economic growth

 III. Multiparty elections

(A) I and II

(B) II and III

(C) I and III

(D) II only

КЪ ВОЙНѢ РОССІИ СЪ ЯПОНІЕЙ.

—Russian image on the upcoming war against Japanese forces in 1904.

390. The image above is best described as an example of

(A) Russian propaganda
(B) Japanese censorship
(C) Russian newspaper editorial
(D) Japanese woodblock print

391. The war between the Russians and Japanese was fought over

(A) Competing ideologies of Russian autocracy versus Japanese democracy
(B) The buffer state of Poland
(C) Territory in China/Manchuria
(D) A disputed election in Russia

—Boys kimono, 1933 courtesy of Sam Perkins

392. The kimono shown above shows clear evidence of which of the following political attitudes prevalent among many Japanese people in the 1930s?

(A) Communism
(B) Industrialism
(C) Militarism
(D) Pacifism

393. The sentiment in Japan as shown in the boy's kimono were fostered by which of the following events?

(A) The economic hardships brought about by the Great Depression
(B) The second Industrial Revolution, which greatly raised living standards
(C) The increased migration of Japanese settlers to the Asian mainland
(D) The spread of pacifist literature and attitudes among college elites

—Photo was taken in 1942/43 in the Pacific campaign against Japanese forces. This photo was censored until after the war.

394. The above photo of dead US marines and damaged landing craft is best understood in the context of the following?

(A) The Pacific theater involved an "island hopping" campaign in light of the region's geography.

(B) The Pacific theater used a Blitzkrieg campaign modeled on its use of tanks in Europe.

(C) The war in the Pacific involved large amounts of US civilian casualties.

(D) The Pacific theater did not use any air power and relied on seagoing forces instead.

395. Similarly to the later US involvement in Vietnam, a difficulty for Allied Forces in the Pacific theater of World War II was

(A) The harsh and long winters that are common to the region

(B) The hostility from the local populations to the Allied cause

(C) The difficult terrain which soldiers had to fight in

(D) The lack of support from their fellow citizens at home

396. The censoring of the preceding photo and other photos during World War II is best understood in the context of which of the following?

(A) World War II was a series of guerilla insurgencies.

(B) World War II was a total war involving civilians.

(C) World War II was a war of ideas such a communism.

(D) World War II was fought for religious reasons.

397. Which policy course did Japanese and German governments take to reverse the economic difficulties of the 1930s?

(A) Stimulation of industry through war preparation

(B) Provision of social insurance through liberal democratic parliamentary means

(C) Worker control of industry

(D) Laissez-faire approach toward economic policy

398. Which element of German fascism was NOT also found in 1930s Japan?

(A) Suspension of parliamentary authority

(B) Ideology of racial supremacy

(C) State-sanctioned mob violence against ethnic minorities

(D) Annexation of nearby territory

399. The United States imposed all of the following elements on Japanese state and society after World War II EXCEPT:

(A) Separation of legislative and executive powers

(B) Strict secular government, banning Shintoism as state religion

(C) Land reform

(D) Banning labor unions

400. Japan's foreign policy in the post–World War II era could be best described as which of the following?

(A) Militarist

(B) Containment

(C) Pacifist

(D) Detente

—Map showing the progress of the Korean War.

401. Using the map, which of the following was the stated goal of the
United States of America in the Korean War?

(A) Contain the spread of Communism
(B) To interfere in the Korean Civil War
(C) To conquer and colonize Korean territory
(D) To maintain the occupation of nearby Japan

402. Korea and Germany were similar in the post–World War II era in that they
were divided. Which of the following provides some context for that?

(A) Both led to a devastating war and ongoing conflict.
(B) Both required the assistance of the United Nations.
(C) Both divisions were due to wartime agreements.
(D) Both divisions were permanent and remain so.

All men are created equal. They are endowed by their Creator with certain inalienable rights; among these are Life, Liberty, and the pursuit of Happiness."
This immortal statement was made in the Declaration of Independence of the United States of America in 1776. In a broader sense, this means: All the peoples on the earth are equal from birth, all the peoples have a right to live, to be happy and free. . . . we, members of the Provisional Government of the Democratic Republic of Vietnam, solemnly declare to the world that Vietnam has the right to be a free and independent country—and in fact is so already. The entire Vietnamese people are determined to mobilize all their physical and mental strength, to sacrifice their lives and property in order to safeguard their independence and liberty.

Source: The Vietnamese Declaration of Independence, which was read by Ho Chi Minh in Hanoi on September 2, 1945.

403. Which of the following statements is a historical argument on the Vietnamese Declaration of Independence shown above that was read out in the city of Hanoi on September 2, 1945?

   (A) The intended audience was the Western powers, especially America, as much as it was the Vietnamese people.
   (B) The Japanese reacted with fury and began to indiscriminately kill Vietnamese intellectuals and professionals.
   (C) The Dutch colonial forces ignored the document and began preparations to regain their former colonial possession.
   (D) The American president Harry Truman issued a strong statement of support for the Vietnamese nationalists.

404. The Vietnamese Declaration of Independence shows the clear influence of

   (A) the Social Darwinist theories that portrayed Asians as inferior to Caucasians
   (B) the nonviolent doctrine of *ahisma* that was used by Mohandas K. Gandhi in India
   (C) Enlightenment principles that were similar to the American Declaration of Independence
   (D) fascist ideals enshrined in Benito Mussolini's 1932 article "What Is Fascism"

Indices of Growth and Change in the Pacific Rim: Gross National Product (GNP), 1965–1996

% Labor Force in Agriculture

% Population Urban

Nation	1965	1996	1965	1996
China	78	72	17	31
Indonesia	66	55	41	82
Japan	20	7	71	78
South Korea	49	18	41	82
Malaysia	54	27	34	54
Thailand	80	64	13	20

—Note: Adapted from World Bank, World Development Indicators (Washington, D.C., 1998).

405. Which of the following is an economic change in Pacific Rim nations from 1965 to 1996 that can be deduced from the chart above?

(A) Pacific nations began to import more than export.

(B) The financial sector had a difficult time raising capital.

(C) More people moved to the countryside than urban areas.

(D) The industrial sector of the Pacific nation's economies grew.

406. Which of the following best explains the cause of the social and economic changes taking place in Pacific nation's from 1965 to 1996?

(A) These nations adopted Marxist Leninist ideologies and communism as an economic system.

(B) These nations industrialized with the exception of Japan, which had begun industrialization earlier.

(C) These nations practiced forced relocation from the countryside to the cities to act as a cheap labor source.

(D) These nations adopted English as an official language and other westernization methods.

407. Based on the chart, which area of the world began to industrialize only in the decades after World War II?

(A) North East Asia

(B) North Africa

(C) South East Asia

(D) Oceania

Population in British Mandate of Palestine, 1922–1945

Year	Total Population	Muslim	Jewish	Christian	Other
1922	752,048	589,177	83,790	71,464	7,617
1931	1,036,339	761,922	175,138	89,134	10,145
1945	1,764,520	1,061,270	553,600	135,550	14,00
Average compounded growth rate per annum, 1922–1945	3.8%	2.6%	8.6%	2.8%	2.7%

408. Which best explains the vast increase of Jewish migration to the British Mandate of Palestine in the years from 1922 to 1945?

   (A) Improvements in communication and transportation
   (B) The continuation of Ottoman policy of toleration of non-Turks
   (C) The persecution of Jews in Europe by Nazi Germany
   (D) Changes in the intra-communal relations of the Jewish diaspora

409. Based on the low numbers of Jews compared to Arab Muslims, which historical argument can be made?

   (A) The dispossession of the Palestinians was unjust in the eyes of many people in the world today.
   (B) The Jewish population in Palestine had a low birth rate due to traditional family planning methods.
   (C) Jews were still suffering from wars and persecution in the Classical and Post-classical Eras.
   (D) Muslim inheritance rituals encouraged the birth of many children, hence a high birth rate.

The Middle East Before and After World War I Settlements, 1914–1922

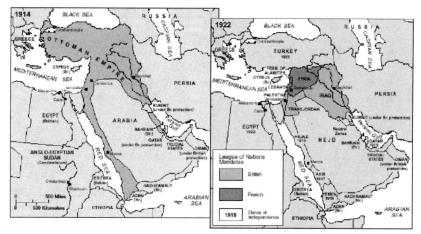

—Map of the Middle East after World War I.

410. Which statement best explains what the map shows?

(A) The impact of the Allied victory in World War I

(B) The rise of nationalist movements in former colonies and territories

(C) The enactment of Wilson's principle of self-determination

(D) The success of the Central Powers at the Paris Peace Conference

411. How does the map reflect the broken promises to Arabs?

(A) The divisions eliminated the possibility of future nationalist movements in the Middle East and North Africa.

(B) They had been promised self-rule, not a mandate system, if they fought with the Allies in the war.

(C) The divisions violated the existing principles of Pan-Arabism, or the unification of all Arab lands.

(D) They had been promised colonies of their own from which to repair their war-torn economies.

"It is no use for you to argue," Talaat answered, "we have already disposed of three quarters of the Armenians; there are none at all left in Bitlis, Van, and Erzeroum. The hatred between the Turks and the Armenians is now so intense that we have got to finish with them. If we don't, they will plan their revenge." "If you are not influenced by humane considerations," I replied, "think of the material loss. These people are your business men. They control many of your industries. They are very large tax-payers. What would become of you commercially without them?" "We care nothing about the commercial loss," replied Talaat. "We have figured all that out and we know that it will not exceed five million pounds. We don't worry about that. I have asked you to come here so as to let you know that our Armenian policy is absolutely fixed and that nothing can change it. We will not have the Armenians any-where in Anatolia. They can live in the desert but nowhere else."

I still attempted to persuade Talaat that the treatment of the Armenians was destroying Turkey in the eyes of the world, and that his country would never be able to recover from this infamy. "You are making a terrible mistake," I said, and I repeated the statement three times. "Yes, we may make mistakes," he replied, "but"—and he firmly closed his lips and shook his head—"we never regret.

—Henry Morgenthau's conversation with Mehmed Talaat, the Turkish Minister of the Interior in 1915 during World War I, recalled for his book, *Ambassador Morgenthau's Story, 1918.*

412. The situation in the reading above is clear evidence of which of the following conclusions?

   (A) Turkish elites were financially supportive of Armenian immigration to South or North America.

   (B) Turkish elites were rightly concerned about economic repercussions that would follow their actions.

   (C) Turkish elites were motivated by a feeling of scientific superiority that placed the Armenians as subhuman.

   (D) Turkish elites knowingly committed acts of genocide against a minority ethnic group within their empire.

413. Which of the following long-term causes most directly led to the actions described in the reading above question 412?

   (A) New technology being used to develop deadlier weapons

   (B) The formation of the Triple Entente Alliance system

   (C) Rising nationalism among various ethnic groups

   (D) The European Mandate system in the Middle East

414. Compared to the German apologies for the Holocaust after World War II, the current Turkish government

(A) Denies a genocide of Armenians took place at all
(B) Has apologized and paid restitution to survivors
(C) Refuses to pay damages to Jews for the crimes
(D) Has been the subject of controversy over its textbooks

> *Among our forefathers were those who maintained that the land of Islam is the fatherland of all Muslims. However, that is a colonialist formula used to advantage by every colonizing nation that seeks to expand its possessions and to extend its influence daily over neighboring countries. Today the [traditional Islamic] formula has no reason to exist. We must replace this formula with the only doctrine that is in accord with every Eastern nation that possesses a clearly defined sense of fatherland. That doctrine is nationalism. Our love of Egypt must be free from all conflicting associations. We must suppress our propensity for anything other than Egypt because patriotism, which is love of fatherland, does not permit such ties. Our Egyptian-ness demands that our fatherland be our qibla* and that we not turn our face to any other.*
> **Marks the direction of Mecca, to which a Muslim turns in prayer.*

> —Ahmad Lutfi as-Sayyid, founder of the Egyptian People's Party in
> 1907, *Memoirs*, Egypt, 1965.

415. Which of the following was a continuity in the Middle East and can be seen in the account above?

(A) The colonization of Egypt by European powers
(B) A debate on the proper role of Islam in government
(C) The love of fatherland by the citizens of the Middle East
(D) The switch from nationalism to socialism in economics

416. Which shift across the Middle East has been taking place from the 1970s and continuing until today?

(A) From socialism to nationalism
(B) From Islamism to nationalism
(C) From nationalism to Islamism
(D) From communism to Islamism

The Security Council,

- *Expressing its continuing concern with the grave situation in the Middle East,*
- *Emphasizing the inadmissibility of the acquisition of territory by war and the need to work for a just and lasting peace in which every State in the area can live in security,*
- *Emphasizing further that all Member States in their acceptance of the Charter of the United Nations have undertaken a commitment to act in accordance with Article 2 of the Charter,*
- *Affirms that the fulfillment of Charter principles requires the establishment of a just and lasting peace in the Middle East which should include the application of both the following principles:*

   1. *Withdrawal of Israeli armed forces from territories occupied in the recent conflict;*

   2. *Termination of all claims or states of belligerency and respect for and acknowledgement of the sovereignty, territorial integrity and political independence of every State in the area and their right to live in peace within secure and recognized boundaries free from threats or acts of force*

—United Nations Resolution 242, November 22, 1967

417. The resolution above by the United Nations supports which of the following conclusions?

(A) Israel in conjunction with Britain and France seized the Suez Canal from Egypt in 1956.

(B) Nuclear proliferation in the Middle East is of the highest concern and must be approved by the Security Council.

(C) The communal violence between Sunni and Shia Muslims must end and all land seized must be returned.

(D) The lands (West Bank, Gaza Strip, and East Jerusalem) seized by Israel are not accepted by the world community.

418. The Arab-Israeli conflict has changed since United Nations Resolution 242 in all of the following ways EXCEPT:

(A) From nationalist divisions to one of religious divisions

(B) From wars between states to one of numerous terrorist acts

(C) From small-scale guerilla war to one of devastating total war

(D) From threats of conventional weapons to threats of nuclear weapons

419. Which British individual indicated support for the creation of a Jewish homeland in Palestine during World War I?

(A) Arthur Balfour
(B) Winston Churchill
(C) Theodor Herzl
(D) Neville Chamberlain

420. Which of the following is NOT a trend or event associated with developments in post–World War II Egypt?

(A) Expulsion of the British from the Suez Canal Zone
(B) Construction of the Aswan dam
(C) Growth of Islamic fundamentalism
(D) Successful import-substitution industrialization

421. Which of the following statements about the Iranian Revolution of 1979 is most accurate?

(A) It marked the end of British colonialism in Iran.
(B) It overthrew a monarchy and installed a liberal democracy.
(C) It was guided by a non-Western ideology.
(D) It was welcomed by neighboring nations.

422. Which natural resource or crop have developing nations been able to trade in the global economy on terms most favorable to themselves?

(A) Cocoa
(B) Coffee
(C) Oil
(D) Diamonds

—Soviet helicopter-tank operation in Afghanistan.
—Afghan warriors or-Mujahideen with two captured Soviet field guns, 1984.

423. The Soviet invasion in 1979, led to which of the following conditions in Afghanistan?

    (A) The stabilization of government, economy, and society

    (B) Industrialization under a socialist command economy

    (C) The opening up of trade relations with the outside world

    (D) A protracted conflict and the emergence of a power vacuum

424. This conflict has often been called the Soviet Union's "Vietnam" due to all of the following EXCEPT:

    (A) The aspect of a guerilla insurgence versus a modern army

    (B) The defeat and withdrawal of the major superpowers' forces

    (C) The difficulty in fighting in jungle terrain and rice fields

    (D) The lack of support for and disillusionment among Russian soldiers

For the last few decades there has been a rapid decline of the handwoven cloth industry throughout the country on account of the competition of machine manufactures. The machine-made goods imported from abroad are much cheaper and of finer quality. . . . Though many still wear clothing made from cloth woven on handlooms, large numbers of handloom weavers have been abandoning their looms.

—Radhakamal Mukerjee, Indian economist, 1916.

425. Which of the following was a historical argument made by Indians such as Radhakamal Mukerjee above and Jawaharlal Nehru in general?
    (A) Cheap cloth is a benefit for everyone from workers to consumers.
    (B) British imperialism led to the "de-industrialization" of India.
    (C) Machine-made cloth is of better quality than hand-made cloth.
    (D) Agricultural-based societies were "purer" than industrial societies.

426. Which of the following acts as context for the changes occurring in the Indian economy as described by Mukerjee?
    (A) New taxation policies by the Indian National Congress
    (B) The invention of the printing press and caravel ships
    (C) The rise of regionalism rather than ethno-nationalism
    (D) The increased integration of India into the world economy

—Mohandas Gandhi on the Salt March, 1930.

427. The image above shows an example of Gandhi's belief in

(A) The rejection of world opinion

(B) Armed anticolonial rebellion

(C) The practice of civil disobedience

(D) Separate Hindu and Muslim states

428. Which person would probably have most strongly opposed Gandhi's actions shown in the image?

(A) A British military officer stationed in India

(B) The leader of the Indian National Congress

(C) The leader of the Muslim coalition in South Africa

(D) A resident of India seeking independence from Britain

—A refugee special train at Ambala Station during partition of India.

429. The relocation of Hindus and Sikhs from Pakistan to India and Muslims from India to Pakistan between 1945 and 1955 reflects which of the following world historical processes?

(A) The migration of former colonial subjects to imperial capitals

(B) Population resettlement caused by redrawing former colonial borders

(C) The development of ethnic enclaves as these migrants moved for work

(D) The seasonal migration patterns associated with temporary work

430. Which of the following legacies of British colonial rule proved most disruptive in the immediate aftermath of Indian independence?

(A) Education of diverse Indian elites in a common English language

(B) Hindu-Muslim rivalry fostered by colonial divide and rule practices

(C) Establishment of parliamentary democratic norms in government

(D) Toleration of caste distinctions

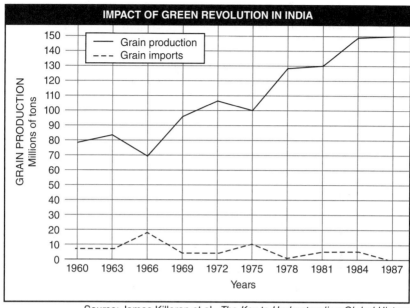

Source: James Killoran et al., *The Key to Understanding Global History*, Jarrett Publishing Co. (adapted)

431. Based on the chart above, the Green Revolution was

(A) A major failure in its goal to produce more food

(B) A benefit to Europe at the expense of Asia and Latin America

(C) A mixed success of larger increases in Mexico than in Pakistan

(D) A major success in its goal of increasing food supply

432. Which of the following is a historical argument about food and India in the Modern Era?

(A) India's success with the Green Revolution has forever ended malnutrition.

(B) India's food staples are exclusively New World crops of potatoes and corn.

(C) India's democratic system has been successful in eliminating famine thus far.

(D) India's nuclear program has come at the expense of its food supply.

1. *The constitution should provide for a Federation of Pakistan in its true sense based on the parliamentary form of government with supremacy of a Legislature directly elected on the basis of universal adult franchise.*

2. *The federal government should deal with only two subjects: Defense and Foreign Affairs, and all other residual subjects should be vested in the federating states.*

3. *Two separate, but freely convertible currencies for two wings should be introduced; or if this is not feasible, there should be one currency for the whole country, but effective constitutional provisions should be introduced to stop the flight of capital from East to West Pakistan. Furthermore, a separate Banking Reserve should be established and separate fiscal and monetary policy be adopted for East Pakistan.*

4. *The power of taxation and revenue collection should be vested in the federating (regional) units and the federal center would have no such power.*

5. *There should be two separate accounts for the foreign exchange earnings of the two wings; the foreign exchange requirements of the federal government should be met by the two wings equally or in a ratio to be fixed; indigenous products should move free of duty between the two wings.*

6. *East Pakistan should have a separate militia or paramilitary force.*

—The Six-Point Program of the Bangladeshi Nationalists, 1966.

433. Which of the following was a short-term result of the Six-Point program listed above?
(A) The partition of India
(B) The withdrawal of British forces
(C) The partition of Pakistan
(D) The first freely held elections

434. Which of the following historical arguments is proven true by the situation in East Pakistan/Bangladesh?
(A) Pakistan is stronger without Bangladesh as a region.
(B) Islam was not enough to overcome other cultural differences.
(C) Chinese aggression was behind the crisis in 1971.
(D) India intended to absorb Bangladesh as a new state.

435. Which of the following accurately summarizes developments in India
since independence?
   I. Maintenance of civilian rule and representative democracy
   II. Growth of a middle class and information technology sector
   III. Elimination of caste distinctions
   IV. Penetration of Green Revolution agricultural techniques down to the
village level
  (A) I and IV
  (B) II and III
  (C) I, II, and III
  (D) I, II, and IV

—Stamp, circa 1938.

436. Which of the following best provides context for the image above?

(A) The Cold War after World War II

(B) European Imperialism in Africa

(C) African colonial troops in World War I

(D) Improved naval technology

437. Which change did the twentieth century see take place in Africa that is reflected in the image?

(A) The demonization of British royalty in African print images

(B) The switch from electronic-based media to paper media

(C) Modern systems of transportation and communication

(D) The draining of Lake Victoria for irrigation purposes

In the twentieth century, and especially since the end of the war, the processes which gave birth to the nation states of Europe have been repeated all over the world. We have seen the awakening of national consciousness in peoples who have for centuries lived in dependence upon some other power. Fifteen years ago this movement spread through Asia. Many countries there, of different races and civilizations, pressed their claim to an independent national life. Today the same thing is happening in Africa, and the most striking of all the impressions I have formed since I left London a month ago is of the strength of this African national consciousness. In different places it takes different forms, but it is happening everywhere. The wind of change is blowing through this continent, and whether we like it or not, this growth of national consciousness is a political fact. We must all accept it as a fact, and our national policies must take account of it. Well you understand this better than anyone, . . . here in Africa you have yourselves created a free nation. A new nation. Indeed in the history of our times yours will be recorded as the first of the African nationalists. This tide of national consciousness which is now rising in Africa, is a fact, for which both you and we, and the other nations of the western world are ultimately responsible.

Source: This speech was made in 1960 by British Prime Minister to the South African Parliament, which had achieved independence from Britain in 1910.

438. The speech above is best understood in the context of

(A) The aftermath of World War II

(B) The Cold War between the US and USSR

(C) South African Apartheid policy

(D) The Spanish Influenza pandemic

439. The "winds of change" that the Prime Minister speaks of resulted in which of the following changes?

(A) The growth in communist ideology amongst Africans

(B) The use of trade winds for the new economies

(C) Many newly independent nations in Africa

(D) The end of the slave trade amongst Islamic nations

440. Although this speech was made in the South Africa parliament, it was ignored by the white settlers since they had a policy of

(A) Containment

(B) Apartheid

(C) Laissez faire

(D) Assimilation

Circa 1960 to 1990.

441. The sign above indicates which continuity in South Africa from the European colonial period the end of the twentieth century?

   (A) The use of Dutch language by English speaking Africans
   (B) The persistence of racist policies by white-dominated governments
   (C) The migration of Dutch settlers to Southern Africa
   (D) The spread of communist ideas in West Africa

442. Which of the following was one result of the effort to end Apartheid in South Africa?

   (A) Apartheid still continues to this day.
   (B) It encouraged the spread of Apartheid.
   (C) It was ineffective in ending Apartheid.
   (D) Apartheid is no longer practiced in South Africa.

443. Why was South Africa's independence struggle atypical when compared with most other African nations?

   (A) Few other African nations gained independence in the 1960s.
   (B) South Africa embarked on a program of rapid state-directed industrialization soon after achieving independence.
   (C) Independence was negotiated by a South African government that consisted of white settlers only.
   (D) South Africa nationalized gold and diamond mines and directed profits from their operation into development projects to lift the standard of living of the black majority there.

444. Which was the most typical response of nationalist leaders in developing countries to popular unrest connected to persistent poverty and/or ethnic strife?

(A) Requests for the return of Western colonial management
(B) A turn to military dictatorship
(C) Free and fair elections of new leaders capable of resolving major grievances
(D) Establishment of new international borders to appease minority ethnicities

445. Which West African nation boasts the continent's largest population and substantial oil reserves?

(A) Senegal
(B) Ghana
(C) Ethiopia
(D) Nigeria

446. How did the independence movement in colonial settler societies such as Algeria or Kenya differ from that in non-settler societies?

(A) In non-settler societies the independence struggle was more likely to turn violent.
(B) In settler societies constructive negotiations tended to yield to power-sharing government coalitions between settlers and representatives of the indigenous populations.
(C) Non-settler societies experienced a smooth transition to independence with steady economic growth and rising per capita incomes based on healthy industrial sectors put in place by colonial administrators.
(D) In settler societies the independence struggle was more likely to turn violent.

February 13 [1905]

DEAR SISTER: . . . And now I inform you that I have very good work. I have been working for 3 months. I have very good and easy work. I earn $8.00 a week. Brother has work also, And as to Brylska, I don't know how she is getting on, and I don't think about her at all. Inform me what is going on in our country, who has come to America, and who got married, and what is the talk in our country about revolution and war, because I have paid for a newspaper for a whole year and the paper comes to me twice a week, so they write that in our country there is misery. They say that in Warsaw and Petersburg there is a terrible revolution and many people have perished already. As to the money, I cannot help you now, sister. You will excuse me yourself, I did not work for five months. . . .

ADAM RACZKOWSKI

—"American letter."

—Advertisement from 1908.

447. The so-called "American letter" on the previous page puts forth which viewpoint about immigration to the Americas in the early 20th century?

(A) The only destination for migrants was America.
(B) "Push-pull" factors were key motivations for migration.
(C) Visas were necessary for entry into nations.
(D) Paper letters were rarely used by the migrants.

448. Based on the image on the previous page, immigration to the Americas was promoted from which areas of the world?

(A) Other regions within the Americas
(B) Europe especially ones with cultural ties
(C) East Asian nations, particularly the Philippines
(D) African nations with Portuguese colonial ties

While conditions in Nicaragua and the action of this government pertaining thereto have in general been made public, I think the time has arrived for me officially to inform the Congress more in detail of the events leading up to the present disturbances and conditions which seriously threaten American lives and property, endanger the stability of all Central America, and put in jeopardy the rights granted by Nicaragua to the United States for the construction of a canal.

It is well known that in 1912 the United States intervened in Nicaragua with a large force and put down a revolution, and that from that time to 1925 a legation guard of American Marines was, with the consent of the Nicaragua government, kept in Managua to protect American lives and property. In 1923 representatives of the five Central American countries, namely, Costa Rica, Guatemala, Honduras, Nicaragua, and Salvador, at the invitation of the United States, met in Washington and entered into a series of treaties.

—Calvin Coolidge, Intervention in Nicaragua, 1925.

449. Which of the following represents a continuity in Latin America from the post-Independence era till today?

(A) The United States has not been interested in economic investment in Latin America.

(B) United States presidents often invited representatives from Cuba and Nicaragua to summits in Washington.

(C) The perception of the United States as a powerful but overbearing neighbor.

(D) Latin American nations were allied closely with their former colonial masters.

450. Which of the following is true regarding US and Latin American relations in the Inter-war Era (1919–1941)?

(A) The United States was nervous about communist aggression in the Andean nations of Peru and Ecuador.

(B) The policy of isolationism applied more to European affairs than Latin American affairs.

(C) Latin American nations formed a single economic union to compete with the United States.

(D) Nations rallied to Nicaragua's side and declared war on the United States in 1930.

—1930s era mural in the town hall of the Mexican city of Valladolid.

451. The causes of the Mexican Revolution of 1910 to 1920 were mainly based on which of the following?

(A) The grievances of the poor and vulnerable

(B) The injuries done to the Catholic Church

(C) The spread of Bolshevik ideas from Russia

(D) The rise of Mexican nationalism

452. In comparison to the Chinese Revolution of 1910, the Mexican Revolution also

(A) overthrew a long-ruling monarchical dynasty

(B) was caused by anger over foreign domination

(C) resulted from the sale and use of opium

(D) led to the establishment of communism

—Female volunteers in the British army from the Caribbean, 1944.

453. The image shown above best demonstrates which of the following conclusions?

  (A) Suffrage was granted to women for their participation in World War II.
  (B) War-related factory work was the only employment that women could acquire.
  (C) Women were encouraged to take part in frontline combat positions.
  (D) Total War requires the active involvement of the civilian population.

454. Which of the following was a direct result of the participation of Caribbean-Americans and other non-white colonial peoples in Europe and Canada in World War II?

  (A) A non-aligned stance during the Cold War
  (B) A push for racial justice and civil rights
  (C) Being suspected of communist sympathies
  (D) A call for more environmental protections

455. How are the nations of Latin America unique within the non-industrialized nations ?

(A) They have struggled to emerge from a dependent role in the global economy.

(B) They have experienced civil war in the post–World War II era.

(C) They gained political independence in the nineteenth century, in general.

(D) They continue to use a language imposed by colonial administrators in internal state affairs.

456. Which independent developing-country regime entered what is best termed as a dependent economic relationship with the Soviet Union that lasted until the collapse of the USSR in the early 1990s?

(A) Ghana

(B) Egypt

(C) India

(D) Cuba

457. Which is the most common pattern of migration in the Americas today?

(A) From North America into Latin America

(B) From Latin American countryside to Latin American cities

(C) From Latin American cities into the Latin American countryside

(D) From Latin America into North America

458. Which global trend had a significant impact in Latin America in the 1930s and 1940s?

   I. Slumping demand for raw materials on world markets

  II. Growing influence of fascism

 III. Independence struggles in colonized regions

(A) I only

(B) I and II

(C) I and III

(D) II and III

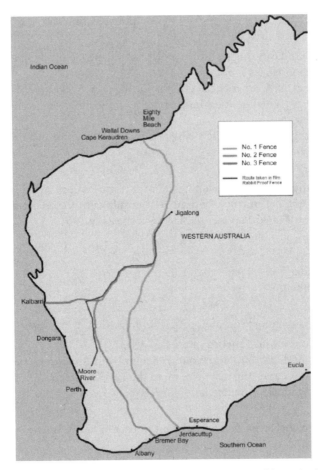

—Map of Western Australia showing the rabbit proof fence built in 1907 but left to ruin by the 1950s.

459. The map showing Australia's rabbit proof fence demonstrates which of the following conclusions?

(A) Rabbits have long inhabited the continent of Australia.

(B) Mammals can be eradicated through rifles and traps.

(C) The environmental impact of European settlements

(D) Sea walls would also have helped with rabbits and rodents.

460. Which of the following is a continuity of world history that can be safely made that is related to Australia's rabbit proof fence?

(A) In the long run walls or barriers are often ineffective.

(B) Australia was geographically isolated for centuries.

(C) Rabbits do not breed or reproduce particularly fast.

(D) Human contact has rarely been a driver of history.

Indian soldiers in the British armed forces in World War I trenches in France, 1915

461. The image above is best understood in the context of

(A) The global nature of World War I due to imperialism
(B) The division of the world into Muslim and Non-Muslim
(C) The spread of nationalist sentiment before World War I
(D) The ending of nonviolent protest among Indians

462. By comparison, World War I differed from World War II in which of the following ways?

(A) World War II was a more limited geographical conflict.
(B) World War II was more mobile in its type of warfare.
(C) World War II was less destructive in terms of civilians.
(D) World War II resulted in a period of stability in China.

—World War I Poster for the Young Women's Christian Association, 1917.

463. The poster above is best understood in the context of

(A) Suffrage movement that demanded votes for women

(B) Total war mobilizing the civilian population

(C) New birth control methods that freed mothers from unplanned pregnancies

(D) Germany's Nazi propaganda machine

464. Which of the following events happened partly as a result of the actions portrayed in the poster?

(A) The Bolshevik Revolution in Russia

(B) The Great Depression

(C) Women achieved suffrage after World War I in the United States and Britain

(D) Germany declared war on Serbia in 1914

Turning and turning in the widening gyre
The falcon cannot hear the falconer;
Things fall apart; the centre cannot hold;
Mere anarchy is loosed upon the world,
The blood-dimmed tide is loosed, and everywhere
The ceremony of innocence is drowned;
The best lack all conviction, while the worst
Are full of passionate intensity.

—"The Second Coming" (1st stanza), by William Butler Yeats, 1919.

465. Which of the following best explains the context behind the poem above?
   (A) An emotional hardening back to a mythological age of heroes
   (B) Feelings of deep anxiety and fear in the post-World War I era
   (C) A rational appeal for a more scientific approach to humanity
   (D) A classic interpretation of the correct behavior for family members

466. The lines "things fall apart; the center cannot hold" makes reference to which historical change?
   (A) The Great Depression and its devastating unemployment problem
   (B) The assassination of the Archduke Ferdinand of Austria-Hungary
   (C) The failure of the League of Nations to solve the Ethiopian crisis
   (D) The fall of some monarchies and challenges to traditional elites

. . . For Fascism, the growth of empire, that is to say the expansion of the nation, is an essential manifestation of vitality, and its opposite a sign of decadence. Peoples which are rising, or rising again after a period of decadence, are always imperialist; and renunciation is a sign of decay and of death. Fascism is the doctrine best adapted to represent the tendencies and the aspirations of a people, like the people of Italy, who are rising again after many centuries of abasement and foreign servitude. But empire demands discipline, the coordination of all forces and a deeply felt sense of duty and sacrifice: this fact explains many aspects of the practical working of the regime, the character of many forces in the State, and the necessarily severe measures which must be taken against those who would oppose this spontaneous and inevitable movement of Italy in the twentieth century, . . .

—*What Is Fascism*, Benito Mussolini, 1932.

467. Based on the above reading, which of the following actions was justified according to the precepts of fascism?

(A) The anti-Semitic policies of Fascist Italy
(B) The Italian invasion of Ethiopia
(C) The Axis alliance with Germany and Japan
(D) The surrender of Italy in 1943 when the Allies invaded

468. Which of the following nations followed a similar foreign policy as fascist Italy in the Interwar Era?

(A) Soviet Union
(B) France
(C) Japan
(D) Mexico

—German school map of Europe, circa 1930s.

Staat	Heeresstärke	
	im Frieden	voraussichtlich im Kriege
Deutschland . . .	100 000	100 000
Albanien	13 000	30 000
Belgien	71 760	600 000
Bulgarien	20 000	20 000
Dänemark	wechselnd bis 26 000	150 000
Estland	14 000	120 000
Finnland	26 000	300 000
Frankreich	655 490	5 000 000
Griechenland . .	66 136	600 000
Großbritannien .	240 000[1]	2 000 000
Irland	14 927	?
Italien	417 000	5 000 000
Jugoslawien . . .	wechselnd bis 140 000	2 000 000
Lettland	23 500	150 000
Litauen	17 800	200 000
Niederlande . . .	35 000	300 000
Norwegen	wechselnd bis 30 000	110 000
Österreich	30 000	30 000
Polen	300 000	3 600 000
Portugal	67 000	870 000
Rumänien	255 000	2 000 000
Rußland	wechselnd bis 1 250 000	7 000 000
Schweden	wechselnd bis 57 000	400 000
Schweiz	wechselnd bis 35 000	400 000
Spanien	175 000	1 800 000
Tschechoslowakei	180 000	1 500 000
Türkei	150 000	1 500 000
Ungarn	35 000	35 000

[1] einschl. 61 000 in Indien

—Detail of map above showing size of European nations armed forces.

Photo by Sean McManamon

469. Based on the preceding German school map, which of the following comparisons is true?

(A) Germany was allowed to build up its armed forces to levels reached by its former enemies.

(B) Germany was smaller than most of its neighboring countries with the exception of France.

(C) Germany was demilitarized after World War I while nations like France, Russia, and Poland built up their armed forces.

(D) Germany expanded its territory after World War I at the expense of its neighbors like France.

470. Which historical argument is supported by the map used in German schools in the Interwar Era (1919–1939)?

(A) Germany surrendered on the battlefield in World War I and formally at the Treaty of Versailles.

(B) Germany was barely affected by the provisions of the Treaty of Versailles.

(C) Germany was able to gain much territory and concessions at the Treaty of Versailles.

(D) Germany was unfairly treated by the Allied powers at the Treaty of Versailles.

Dates of the Great Depression

Country	Depression Began	Recovery Began	Decline in industrial production during the Great Depression
United States	mid-1929	mid-1933	47%
Germany	early 1928	mid-1932	42%
Italy	mid-1929	early 1933	33%
France	mid-1930	mid-1932	31%
United Kingdom	early 1930	late 1932	16%
Japan	early 1930	mid-1932	9%

471. Based on the countries in this table, the decline in industrial production during the Great Depression was relatively more severe in countries
   (A) That had industrialized more recently
   (B) That had large overseas colonial empires
   (C) Where the Great Depression began earlier
   (D) Where World War I battles had been fought

472. Which is the most important reason why Germany suffered so severely from the Great Depression?
   (A) The refusal of the Soviets to repay war debt to Germany and Austria.
   (B) The economic disruptions due to the provisions of the Versailles treaty.
   (C) The billions of dollars in war reparations that France owed to Germany.
   (D) The printing of less paper money in Germany, causing deflation.

Through our protective measures of 13 August 1961 we have only safeguarded and strengthened that frontier which was already drawn years ago and made into a dangerous front-line by the people in Bonn and West Berlin. How high and how strongly fortified a frontier must be, depends, as is common knowledge, on the kind of relations existing between the states of each side of the frontier ... We no longer wanted to stand by passively and see how doctors, engineers, and skilled workers were induced by refined methods unworthy of the dignity of man to give up their secure existence here and work in West Germany or West Berlin.

—The following is the text of a 1962 brochure from the German Democratic Republic (GDR) It was published in English for foreign distribution.

There are many people in the world who really don't understand, or say they don't, what is the great issue between the free world and the Communist world. Let them come to Berlin. There are some who say that communism is the wave of the future. Let them come to Berlin. Freedom has many difficulties and democracy is not perfect, but we have never had to put a wall up to keep our people in, to prevent them from leaving us...Freedom is indivisible, and when one man is enslaved, all are not free. When all are free, then we can look forward to that day when this city will be joined as one and this country and this great Continent of Europe in a peaceful and hopeful globe. When that day finally comes, as it will, the people of West Berlin can take sober satisfaction in the fact that they were in the front lines for almost two decades. All free men, wherever they may live, are citizens of Berlin, and, therefore, as a free man, I take pride in the words "Ich bin ein Berliner."

—President John F. Kennedy's speech in June, 1963 when he visited Berlin.

473. The readings above are best understood in the context of which of the following historical events?

(A) The Rise of Islamic Fundamentalism
(B) The Cold War years
(C) The European Union
(D) The increase in illegal migration

474. The second reading by President Kennedy differs from the first reading from the GDR in that it

(A) takes a stand against illegal immigration to Berlin
(B) agrees that the Berlin Wall is keeping the peace
(C) opposes the Berlin Wall as antithetical to freedom
(D) supports the communist idea of a divided Berlin

THE WAY BACK

—Political cartoon.

475. The Marshall Plan was developed to

(A) Create a tariff-free Common Market in Europe
(B) Rebuild the economies of Europe after World War II
(C) Bring about the unification of Europe
(D) Increase Europe's dependence on the United States

476. Which was a strong motivation for the Marshall Plan in Europe?

(A) The return of the Nazi party in England and Germany
(B) The fall of the Berlin Wall and reunification of Germany
(C) Fear of economic hardships leading to extremist politics
(D) The Vietnam War effects on domestic opinion in Germany

477. Why were Great Britain and France able to insulate themselves from the Great Depression to a greater extent than Germany or the United States?
   (A) By 1929, industrial production was no longer central to their national economies.
   (B) Both nations unloaded a certain amount of surplus industrial production on markets in their extensive colonial holdings.
   (C) Strong labor movements in both countries refused to accept layoffs.
   (D) Britain and France were able to collect on loans made to Germany.

478. Which of the following was the first group targeted by the Nazis for repression once they seized power in Germany?
   (A) Jews
   (B) Communists
   (C) Gypsies
   (D) Homosexuals

479. The North Atlantic Treaty Organization (NATO) and the Warsaw Pact are most accurately described as
   I. Free trade zones
   II. Collective security organizations
   III. Colonial holdings
   (A) I and II
   (B) II and III
   (C) I and III
   (D) II only

480. Which of the following best characterizes developments in the societies of Western Europe in the decades after World War II?
   I. Expanding welfare state provisions
   II. Steady economic growth
   III. Broad enthusiasm for expansion of colonial holdings
   (A) I only
   (B) I and II
   (C) I and III
   (D) II only

EXTREMISTS' RISE TO POWER IN RUSSIA

From Outset of Revolution They Have Thwarted Efforts of Moderate Governments.

SAPPED KERENSKY'S RULE

Supported Premier Only When the Korniloff Movement Filled Them with Apprehension.

—New York Times headline November 9th, 1917.

481. The issues referred to in the headlines above is best understood in the context of

(A) World War I
(B) the rise of fascism
(C) the Russian Revolution
(D) the Great Depression

482. It can plausibly be argued that the seizure of power in Russia by radical socialists and communists in 1917 marks the beginning of

(A) The Mandate System
(B) The Cold War
(C) World War I
(D) The League of Nations

The famine of 1932–1933 was the most terrible and destructive that the Ukrainian people have ever experienced. The peasants ate dogs, horses, rotten potatoes, the bark of trees, grass—anything they could find. Incidents of cannibalism were not uncommon. The people were like wild beasts, ready to devour one another. And no matter what they did, they went on dying, dying, dying. . . .

There was no one to gather the bumper crop of 1933, since the people who remained alive were too weak and exhausted. More than a hundred persons—office and factory workers from Leningrad—were sent to assist on the kolkhoz; two representatives of the Party arrived to help organize the harvesting. . . .

That summer (1933) the entire administration of the kolkhoz—the bookkeeper, the warehouseman, the manager of the flour mill, and even the chairman himself—were put on trial on charges of plundering the kolkhoz property and produce. All the accused were sentenced to terms of seven to ten years, and a new administration was elected. . . .

—*The History of a Soviet Collective Farm* by Fedor Belov.

483. Which of the following acts as context for the reading above?
   (A) The problems of totalitarian rule in the Soviet Union
   (B) The over reliance on agriculture as a food source
   (C) The damage done by the Nazi German invasion
   (D) The dangers of the Cold War between the superpowers

484. Which Soviet policy contributed greatly to the tragedy described above?
   (A) De-Stalinization
   (B) Glasnost
   (C) Collectivization
   (D) Detente

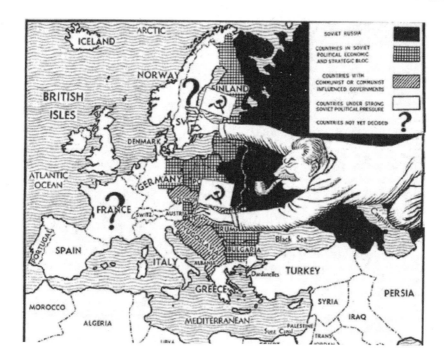

485. After World War II, the Soviet Union established satellites in Eastern Europe in order to achieve which of the following?

(A) Support the remaining Fascist governments in Eastern Europe

(B) Preserve entrepreneurship in Eastern Europe

(C) Create a buffer against future invasion from the West

(D) Establish democratic governments in Eastern European nations

486. One major cause of the Cold War was the

(A) Trade competition between imperial powers

(B) Differences in ideology between the United States and the USSR

(C) Differences in how to best promote literacy throughout the world

(D) Determination of the United States to maintain political control of Eastern Europe

Soviet propaganda poster issued in Uzbekistan, 1933, "Strengthen working discipline in collective farms"

487. Based on the image above, the Soviet Union instituted which of the following changes?

(A) The implementation of communist economic policies in rural areas

(B) The banishment of refugees from Central Asia to Eastern Europe

(C) The increase in population through centralized family planning

(D) The ending of payments to the old aristocracy from czarist Russia

488. Based on the image above, which of the following was a commonality of totalitarian regimes in the twentieth century?

(A) Use of the elderly as a revolutionary force

(B) Television and radio propaganda

(C) Private ownership of industry and factories

(D) Persecution of minorities and scapegoats

A Comparison of Work Time Needed to Buy Goods and Services in the United States and Soviet Union, 1982

Goods and Services	Soviet Union	United States
White Bread (2.2 pounds)	17 minutes	16 minutes
Sirloin Steak (2.2 pounds)	182 minutes	79 minutes
Chicken (2.2 pounds)	185 minutes	16 minutes
Fresh Milk (1 quart)	22 minutes	6 minutes
Potatoes (2.2 pounds)	7 minutes	7 minutes
Oranges (2.2 pounds)	92 minutes	10 minutes
Bath Soap	20 minutes	4 minutes
Aspirin	246 minutes	5 minutes
Lipstick	69 minutes	30 minutes
Gasoline (3 gallons)	210 minutes	36 minutes
Newspaper	3 minutes	3 minutes
Blue Jeans	46 hours	3 hours
Washing Machine	165 hours	47 hours
Gas Bill (1 month)	39 minutes	290 minutes
Telephone Call (local)	1 minute	2 minutes
Haircut	37 minutes	63 minutes
Car (medium sized)	88 months	8 months
Rent (1 month)	12 hours	56 hours

—Radio Library Research Supplement, 1982.

489. Based on the chart above, which of the following conclusions can be made about the Soviet Union compared to the United States?

(A) Trade goods were imported from wealthy Western countries.
(B) Basics necessities were more affordable than consumer goods.
(C) Goods like aspirin were within easy reach of all Soviet citizens.
(D) The costs of a newspaper and magazines was vastly different.

490. Which of the following was a result in the Soviet Union of the conditions outlined in the chart above?

(A) Economic stagnation and shortages of consumer goods
(B) Trade tariffs and other barriers to interaction with the world
(C) An increase in the world price of petroleum and heating gas
(D) A rise in the standard of living for workers and peasants

491. Which term do historians employ to describe both Hitler's Germany and Stalin's USSR?

(A) Fascist
(B) Communist
(C) Totalitarian
(D) Democratic

492. Which of the following were offered by the Stalin regime as reasons to pursue collectivization of agriculture and Five-Year Plans in industry after 1928?

I. Reversal of the NEP and inculcation of socialist habits among the Soviet masses
II. Reduction of the Soviet population to environmentally sustainable levels
III. Rapid industrialization to prepare for a second imperialist invasion of the USSR

(A) I only
(B) I and II
(C) II and III
(D) I and III

493. Which socialist Eastern European nation was not a Soviet satellite state?

(A) Romania
(B) Hungary
(C) East Germany
(D) Yugoslavia

494. Which best characterizes weaknesses of the Soviet economy after World War II?

I. Inflexible central planning
II. Low worker morale and productivity
III. Raw-material shortages

(A) I and II
(B) II and III
(C) I and III
(D) I only

495. Which Soviet leader was a leading force in imposing economic, diplomatic, and political reforms after 1985 that contributed directly to the demise of Soviet socialism?

(A) Nikolay Bukharin
(B) Leonid Brezhnev
(C) Mikhail Gorbachev
(D) Nikita Khrushchev

"Russians" (song & lyrics by Sting)

In Europe and America, there's a growing feeling of hysteria
Conditioned to respond to all the threats
In the rhetorical speeches of the Soviets
Mr. Khrushchev* said we will bury you
I don't subscribe to this point of view
It would be such an ignorant thing to do
If the Russians love their children too

How can I save my little boy from Oppenheimer's deadly toy**
There is no monopoly in common sense
On either side of the political fence
We share the same biology
Regardless of ideology
Believe me when I say to you
I hope the Russians love their children too

There is no historical precedent
To put the words in the mouth of the President
There's no such thing as a winnable war
It's a lie we don't believe anymore
Mr. Reagan*** says we will protect you
I don't subscribe to this point of view
Believe me when I say to you
I hope the Russians love their children too

We share the same biology
Regardless of ideology
What might save us, me, and you
Is if the Russians love their children too

*Russia's leader in the 1950s & 1960s
** The atomic bomb
***America's leader in the 1980s

496. Which of the following provides historical context for the lyrics above to the song "Russians"?
   (A) The United States' policy of containment of communism
   (B) The arms race between the United States and the USSR
   (C) The use of science in the Green Revolution
   (D) The friendship of Communist Russia and China

497. References to lyrics like "there's no such thing as a winnable war" refer to which aspect of the Cold War?
   (A) NATO or North America Treaty Organization
   (B) DMZ or demilitarized zone
   (C) MAD or mutually assured destruction
   (D) SALT or Strategic Arms Limitation Agreement

498. The Green Revolution was largely in response to which of the following developments in the Postwar Era?
   (A) Tensions between the East and the West during the Cold War
   (B) High population growth in the so-called Third World
   (C) Increased use of science in weapons technology
   (D) Spread of Old World foods to the New World

499. Which political system, discredited by its inability to effectively prevent economic collapse or a turn to political extremism, emerged triumphant in the post–World War II West?
   (A) Socialism
   (B) Liberal democracy
   (C) Fascism
   (D) Monarchy

500. NAFTA has more closely integrated the economies of Canada, the United States, and
   (A) Russia
   (B) China
   (C) Mexico
   (D) Venezuela

ANSWERS

Chapter 1

1. (A) A court fight over the Treasure Fleet voyages emerged between Confucian scholars who saw little value in them while the court eunuchs promoted them and fellow eunuch Zheng He who led the voyages.

2. (A) The Chinese were reported to have visited the East Coast of Africa and even been given a giraffe as a gift for the Chinese emperor who lived what must have been a lonely life in Beijing.

3. (C) Scholars have divided the study of China into dynasties as a way to understand this civilization. Other East Asian civilizations like Japan are also studied in this way.

4. (B) The Mandate of Heaven was developed in the Classical Era as a way to explain and justify why the ruling dynasties were replaced by other dynasties.

5. (B) During the Song dynasty Chinese cities saw a profusion of trade until the Mongol onslaught in the twelfth century.

6. (C) Confucian tradition teaches that merchants who do not produce anything or govern are little better than parasites and therefore are not respected as a social class.

7. (A) Islam was introduced into China by the eighth century by traders and migrants. X'ian as the endpoint of the Silk Road was a cosmopolitan urban center of Muslim, Christian, and even Jewish communities. The long established contact between Chinese cultures and these newer belief systems encouraged a blending of cultures.

8. (C) Islam established a prescience in some Chinese cities by the eighth century during the Postclassical Era.

9. (C) Scholars and government officials were schooled and tested in Confucian classics, which encourage them to look down on other belief systems.

10. (A) One argument against Buddhism by Confucian scholars was its foreign origin in India. References such as "cult of barbarians" and "did not speak the languages of China" show clear ethnocentrism.

11. (B) Choices (C) and (D) can be eliminated immediately. Looking at the remaining, China maintained generally superior craftsmanship and manufacturing capacity until the Industrial Revolution after the year 1800.

12. (A) Ambitious individuals and their families through test preparation and test taking gained positions of power in the Chinese bureaucracy; other choices may have been true in rare cases but do not rise to the level of being the "best" choice to answer this question.

13. (D) Mongols were more appreciative of trade than were traditional Chinese elites. This was due to a number of factors such as source of taxation, as well as new ideas and needed products from other civilizations.

14. (D) China generated perhaps the largest share of key inventions of the Premodern Era. The rise of the Industrial Revolution in the West changed all that. Steam power dates from eighteenth-century England.

15. (A) This symbol of China's strict patriarchy developed in the Song Dynasty and continued up until the mid-20th century.

16. (B) Many aspects of Chinese culture such as Buddhism, Confucianism, Daoism, and the writing system were introduced to Japan from the fourth to the eighth century.

17. (C) Chinese Mahayana Buddhism was influential in both Korea and Japan.

18. (B) Japan was not politically unified till late in the 16th century. Previously, central Japan was often a battleground for control by various clans.

19. (A) The code of the Japanese warriors was Bushido, which translates as the "way of the warrior." This code was repurposed in the late nineteenth century as Japan embarked on imperialistic ventures in Asia.

20. (B) The Mongol invasions of Japan in 1274 and 1281 failed, and this marked the last time that Japan faced a serious outside threat until the nineteenth century with the arrival of the Americans in 1854.

21. (B) The failed Mongol invasions of Japan later contributed to a Japanese belief in their special role in the world and fear of outsiders in the island nation.

22. (C) The main trend in the postclassical era was for societies to move from a slave-based economic and social structure to one we call feudal. The similarities between European and Japanese feudalism stem in part from the relative isolation from global trade routes (as compared to the Byzantine or Islamic civilizations at the time) and the resultant necessity to base economic activity around cultivation of the land both civilizations shared.

23. (D) Japan did not borrow the civil service exam from China and instead relied upon a social structure based on the rule of a warrior elite.

24. (C) Japanese emperors traditionally had no real power, unlike in China were they wield immense power. In Japan, military leaders known as shoguns governed the nation.

25. (D) India was a great cultural influence on Southeast Asia, which can be seen in its religious traditions, architecture, dance, and writing system.

26. (A) Angkor Wat was originally a Hindu temple complex but was converted to and remains a Buddhist temple complex and monastery.

27. (A) Buddhism, like Christianity, offers the option of a monastic lifestyle as a show of devotion.

28. (B) Mahayana Buddhism was more influential in East Asia including Vietnam whereas most of Southeast Asia was influenced by Theravada Buddhism.

29. ((D) In no region listed did a majority convert to Islam, with the possible exception of Indonesia.

30. (B) A social hierarchy was common to all three and is also key to state formation.

31. (C) Monastic life refers to life in a monastery or, in this case, a nunnery. Monasticism represented one of the few exits for women from the generally restrictive gender roles of family life of the classical and postclassical worlds.

32. (B) During the Abbasid dynasty the Islamic cities of Baghdad and Cordova were great centers of learning, especially scientific learning in astronomy, optics, and navigation.

33. (D) Before the year 1200, Baghdad was perhaps the most sophisticated city on the planet. Only Chinese urban centers would have rivaled it.

34. (A) Networks of caravanserai were stretched over South West Asia/Middle East to provide for the basic needs for traveling merchants and promote overland trade.

35. (C) When the Europeans realized their long-term goal of finding an all-water route to Asia, the Middle East began to slowly lose its profitable role as the middle man. Caravanserai began to diminish in importance.

36. (C) A decrease in the number of workers due to deaths caused the remaining workers to feel empowered to higher wages for their services.

37. (A) Both the Mamluk and European governments realized the contagious nature of the bubonic plague and took steps to quarantine the infected and limit public interactions.

38. (C) A bias toward a European perspective is pervasive throughout many scholarly disciplines, even outside Europe.

39. (B) In East Asia, the study of history is divided into dynastic periods such as the Ming in China, the Tokugawa in Japan, or the Yi in Korea.

40. (C) From a Eurocentric point of view, the beginning of the "Middle Ages" in the Middle East would correspond to that of Europe, which would be the fall of the (Western) Roman empire.

41. (D) In both cases the belief systems of the Byzantines and the Abbasids survived their empire's decline and fall. In fact, Eastern Orthodox Christianity and Islam remained the dominant belief systems in Eastern Europe and Middle East, respectively.

42. (D) Steam power is quintessentially modern and can be traced to eighteenth-century Great Britain. All postclassical civilizations qualify as premodern.

43. (D) Muhammad's retreat to Medina and his triumphant return to Mecca are seminal events in the early spread of the Islamic faith.

44. (D) Silk Roads passed through the Central Asian heartlands of the Mongol Empire.

45. (C) The Mongols conquered the territory that is now Korea, which was for centuries a Chinese tributary state.

46. (D) The image shows Persian or Turkish musicians on the back of a camel that inhabits the western (non-Han Chinese) areas that had long had contact and trade with peoples west of China. The fact that the piece was made in China shows the links between these areas of the world.

47. (A) Camels requiring less water than horses and being built for a desert climate were ideal for transportation.

48. (A) Europeans feared the Mongols as barbarian warriors similar to the Huns who contributed to the fall of the Roman Empire. Descriptions such as Paris's would have solidified this feeling.

49. (D) Marco Polo as a traveler with his father and uncle were accepted as merchants, and his long time in the East had given Marco a positive view of the Mongols as well as other peoples of the East.

50. (C) The Pax Mongolica term is used to describe the eased communication and commerce the unified administration helped to create and the period of relative peace that followed the Mongols' vast conquests.

51. (A) Passports, caravanserai, and border patrols are methods that the state used to promote trade.

52. (B) The Mongols were very open to new ideas from other civilizations whether it was new military technology such as siege machines or religions such as Islam or Tibetan Buddhism.

53. (C) This merit system helped to explain the consistently superior quality of Mongol military forces. Nomadic people, not possessing property in land, are generally less inculcated with a respect for inherited wealth and lineage.

54. (D) The phalanx infantry formation was a Greek military technique where the soldiers aligned in a massive rectangular formation.

55. (C) After the death of Genghis Khan the Mongol Empire was split into a number of khanates. These root-word games may seem trivial now but are important later on in the course, since across the globe nationhood winds up replacing all manner of monarchy and aristocratic rule. *Kingdom, principality, empire,* and *county* are of similar derivation.

56. (B) While Muslims had been in India since the eighth century, they were either in small numbers as raiding parties or merchants in port cities. The Delhi Sultanate was the first permanent Islamic rulers to establish themselves.

57. (C) The towering height of the Qutb Minar and its use of carved stones from nearby Hindu temples were meant to demonstrate the primacy of Islam.

58. (D) Sufism was popular in some areas of the Muslim world, especially in countries where Islam was not overwhelmingly the majority religion. Sufism can be seen as a form of accommodation to different faiths.

59. (B) Sufism is a focus on a spiritual or aesthetic form of Islam rather than on strict doctrines. Sufis are known to dance, sing, and compose poetry. In countries that practice a more fundamentalist form of Islam, Sufis are often outlawed and disowned.

60. (B) This characteristic is more widely recognized by Westerners in Confucian and Hindu traditions than in the Christian tradition. Numerous biblical passages exhort the poor and the slave to accept their lots in life and obey their masters. Choice (A) is false regarding Confucianism.

61. (A) The Indus River valley of northwest India had been a target of imperial conquest from the days of Alexander, and Spain and Morocco were the farthest westward outpost of the old Roman Mediterranean imperium. Islam at its height guided the trade and collected the knowledge of this vast, rich, and ancient zone of civilized humanity.

62. (D) Buddhists carried over the belief in reincarnation from Hinduism.

63. (B) Phrases such as "source of legitimacy for their rule" "gained recognition" and "political alliances" show how political considerations were important in the conversion to Islam. Conversion was of a top-down nature.

64. (A) The phrase in the early part of the excerpt how "They did not . . . give up their religious . . . traditions" shows how Islam coexisted with previous belief systems.

65. (D) Ibn Battuta was an older Islamic jurist who throughout his travel journals demonstrated a critical eye for practices he felt were un-Islamic or communities he felt were less than observant.

66. (A) Ibn Battuta was upset at the casual gender relations and wanted more separation between genders who were not family. Terms like "shocked" and "amazed" demonstrate his displeasure.

67. (A) Prior to the discovery of gold in the Americas, Africa was a key source of gold for Europeans.

68. (C) West Africa was known for its trade of salt for gold in equal amounts due to the geographic disparities in various areas of Africa.

69. (B) Mansa Musa was famous for his journey to the Islamic holy cities of Mecca and Medina and his lavish spending and actions inadvertently devastated the economies of the regions through which he passed.

70. (C) Great Zimbabwe in Southern Africa was a thriving agricultural and trade center in the Postclassical Era but its achievements were later denied by European settlers who claimed it had to have been founded by a Mediterranean society.

71. (D) Like many other famous archaeological sites, Great Zimbabwe was abandoned and the reasons remain unclear. Scholars are still investigating the exact causes, which include shifts in trade routes, political instability, and climate change.

72. (C) Choice (A) is accurate for some but not all of postclassical black Africa. Choices (B) and (D) are not accurate descriptors of the same.

73. (A) Integration of west, central, eastern, and southern Africa into world trade was achieved via Muslim contact as well as trans-Saharan and Indian Ocean trade networks.

74. (D) Ivory is taken mainly from elephant tusks and has been worked by artisans from many civilizations—including African ones. The other listed materials are more associated with Mediterranean civilization (marble, oil paint, mosaic tile) or China (jade).

75. (A) Coptic Christianity has been the state religion in these societies from the days of the Roman Empire up until the present.

76. (D) The Incas developed quipu to keep records, although their exact use is still being investigated.

77. (B) The Incan system for record keeping, called the quipu, was indigenous to the Americas and not influenced by any outside cultures.

78. (A) The Incas' empire was founded in the mountainous city of Cuzco and spread along the Andes Mountains north to Columbia and as far south as Chile.

79. (C) The Incan empire was primarily located in the Andes Mountains. They overcame difficult geography to stretch their empire from the modern nation of Colombia down to Chile.

80. (B) China has long had a number of areas that use terrace or step farming as a way to increase agricultural output for its large population.

81. (D) Potatoes, corn, and beans were the staple crops of the Americas and due to the Columbian Exchange spread to become staple foods in many areas of the world.

82. (B) *Mita* or *corvee* extracts labor from the natives as a form of obligatory public service or tribute.

83. (C) The Aztecs were an aggressive empire who conquered and dominated neighboring states from which they received regular tribute.

84. (A) The Codex Mendoza may not be accurate since it was written two decades after the Spanish conquered the Aztecs.

85. (A) The non-Aztecs peoples will eagerly join the Spanish in defeating their hated overlords.

86. (D) Raids by Aztec military forces into surrounding populations to capture prisoners of war for use in sacrificial ceremonies sowed seeds of resentment that the conquistadors were able to exploit to gain indigenous allies in the conquest of the Aztec city of Tenochtitlan.

87. (C) No large animals appropriate for domestication existed in the "New World." Despite this, Native American civilizations accomplished remarkable degrees of architectural achievements using only human muscle power.

88. (A) The Aztec civilizations centered around a semi-tropical Valley of Mexico with irrigated lake-based agricultural land while Inca civilization radiated out from mountain highlands climatic zones and made use of terrace farming.

89. (C) The Inuit people adapted to Greenland by relying on fish, fowl, and mammal food sources that they could catch or hunt. Their weapons, tools, clothes, and watercraft were carefully engineered for the environment, whereas the Greenland Vikings were better suited to warmer climates and farming.

90. (B) The Greenland Viking settlements died out by the 1400s and scholars still debate the various theories. Some such theories are climate change, the Black Death and the inability to adapt to a new environment.

91. (C) There is no evidence that Austronesian seafarers made it past Easter Island to the west coast of South America.

92. (A) Bantu-speaking peoples dominate much of the southern half of Africa from its origin in West Africa while Austronesian languages spread from Easter Island to Madagascar.

93. (C) The Austronesian outrigger canoe is perfectly suited for island hopping across the Pacific Ocean. Also, their voyages within recent history without charts or navigational tools are awe-inspiring. Furthermore, we have linguistic proof of their ocean prowess.

94. (B) The image of the farmers in the forefront doing agricultural work shows the farming/agricultural basis of the European economy.

95. (D) The images show lords and peasants fulfilling different roles and occupying different levels of society.

96. (B) In return for loyalty and military service, nobles would receive fiefs from their overlords that included land, houses, castles, and serf peasants.

97. (C) The fall of the Western Roman Empire and the lack of a strong centralized government brought about an economic and social system known as feudalism. This was similar to the situation in early Japan where there was no central authority until the Tokugawa shoguns united the country.

98. (B) Japan also developed a feudalistic system of government and social system of daimyo lords and samurai warriors.

99. (B) The chart of Hanseatic League trade clearly shows higher amounts for exports than imports. This demonstrates the League's success.

100. (D) The Hanseatic League trade provided the economic basis for the cultural flowering that sprung from Northern German towns, England and the Low Countries. This was similar to the Mediterranean trade contributing to the Italian Renaissance.

101. (A) The Bubonic Plague caused a labor shortage that put severe stress on the old feudal relationship and ushered in a wage labor system.

102. (D) The Bubonic Plague predates this declaration by three years and the shortage of workers persuaded workers to push for wage laborers.

103. (D) European military outposts lasted several centuries at most. Jerusalem has never been a Christian town, and Islam split into the Sunni and Shia branches in the seventh century (the Crusades were mainly a twelfth-century phenomenon).

104. (D) "High Middle Ages" refers to a period from about 1000 to 1300 and connotes something of a recovery from the Dark Ages that followed the fall of Rome in the fifth century. (A) predates the High Middle Ages, while (B) and (C) occurred after.

105. (C) Even European ruling elites tended to be illiterate in the first centuries after the fall of Rome. Peasant illiteracy is not as surprising perhaps. Monasteries were outposts of reading and writing in this period.

106. (D) Serfdom was the dominant form of labor during the Middle Ages replacing slave labor from the Classical era, especially in Europe.

107. (D) The Byzantine borrowed from the earlier Roman system of both secular authority as well as divine authority. Also, a breakdown of the term *caesaropapism* contain parts that help with its definition.

108. (A) The Byzantine empire was a huge influence on Russian religion, writing system, calendar, architecture, and imperial system.

109. (A) Constantinople was founded by Greek settlers and its had long been a great center of trade and culture due to its location on the Bosporus Straits between the Black and Mediterranean seas dividing Europe from Asia.

110. (B) The Great Schism of 1025 brought a final rupture in the Christian church that had its origins in Roman times when the Empire was divided into Western and Eastern halves and the linguistic differences of Latin and Greek.

111. (D) Russia was forced to pay regular payments of valuable goods to the Golden Horde (Mongols) after being defeated.

112. (A) One of the theories for Russia's relationship with the West is that the long years of Mongol domination caused it to fall behind the West and be removed from key developments and trade.

113. (D) The eastern Mediterranean had been predominantly culturally Greek from the Classical Era and remained so until the arrival of the Ottoman Turks in the fifteenth century CE. The reversion from Latin back to Greek in both church and state affairs after the fall of the Western Roman Empire is evidence of this tendency.

114. (A) Neither Scandinavia, India, nor sub-Saharan Africa is adjacent to the choke point between the Black and Mediterranean Seas that made Byzantium such a key trade hub in the ancient world.

115. (B) Early Russian civilization is known as "Kievan Rus" after the city of Kiev, which ironically today is in the Ukraine.

116. (B) Neither the Byzantines nor the Song dynasty were ruled by female monarchs exclusively. However, the Byzantines occasionally had women emperors and the preceding Tang dynasty did have Empress Wu, but that was the exception rather than the norm.

117. (B) According to scholars, the game of chess originated in India and diffused westward to the Islamic Middle East and North Africa where it was exposed to Europeans there and in Spain.

118. (D) The movement of the Lewis chessmen from Arctic Circle, Norway, and the Hebrides was primarily by sea, which was the quickest way to move goods. The Indian Ocean trade network was well established at this point in history.

119. (C) The Lewis chessmen were carved from walrus tusks and were traded long distances. Only highly prices items were worth the effort of movement over tough environments. Demonstrating the example, are staple foods which were rarely shipped through the North Sea but animal furs were.

120. (B) The argument that the Italian Renaissance was a break with the Postclassical Era and a rebirth of Classical themes was advanced by artists and scholars from the Early Modern Era themselves.

121. (B) Medieval Europeans had a limited understanding of the wider world and that limited knowledge would have been strongly influenced by Christianity.

122. (A) Europeans began to have a wider world view due to the Crusades, increased trade, and early exploration.

123. (C) The map only shows Europe, Africa, and Asia and omits the Americas and Antarctica due to a lack of knowledge of those areas.

124. (D) By 1400 gunpowder weapons are able to knock down castle walls and gates. This will later be proved in 1453 by the Ottoman seizure of Constantinople.

Chapter 2

125. (A) The use of awe-inspiring mountains hidden by mists cut by hidden streams with the diminutive size of humans and the inclusion of poetry in the top left of the painting uses a metaphor of a traveler's journey for a journey of one's life make clear reference to Daoism.

126. (D) Paintings, calligraphy, and poetry, which complement one another, were the provenance of the scholar class in traditional China.

127. (B) The Portuguese were the first Europeans to reach China and they were under strict restrictions based on their outsider status and merchant activities.

128. (A) The Chinese were always suspicious of non-Chinese probably due to their experiences in the northwest frontier where nomadic tribes had long posed a threat. Confucianism also contributed to Chinese ethnocentrism or sinocentrism.

129. (B) The excerpt above undoubtedly written by a Confucian scholar is tolerant of Buddhism and Daoism but is dismissive of the new religion being spread by Christian missionaries.

130. (B) Despite the efforts of Jesuit and other Christian missionaries and the fears of the Chinese elites, Christianity did not take have many followers.

131. (D) The Jesuits was one of the main responses to the threat posed by the Protestant Reformation. Jesuits were highly trained and aggressive In their missionary work.

132. (B) The Jesuits had little initial success in China but when they began to dress in scholar's robes, grow their beards, and learn the Chinese language, they had more success especially with higher classes.

133. (D) Filial piety or respect for one's elders and superiors is one of the main pillars of Confucianism.

134. (A) The Qing dynasty underwent considerable Sinification to appear to Chinese and lessen any resistance to their rule.

135. (D) Multiple factors came into play for this most important "nondecision" in world history.

136. (A) Unlike the Mongols, the Qing (Manchu) rulers relied on Chinese Confucian-trained bureaucrats at almost every level of the bureaucracy. Like the Mongols, the Qing held the top posts in government.

137. (C) East Asia has been the most populous region on earth since the classical era, and that is still the case today.

138. (B) Bullion, or precious metals, was a trade product that Europeans had in increasing amounts because of their control of the New World and it was initially the only commodity that Western merchants had that East Asia merchants and rulers desired on a consistent basis.

139. (C) In 1600, the daimyo Tokugawa Ieyasu was able to establish their domination over the other daimyo contenders and establish their descendants as shoguns. Therefore, the large number of samurai involved in the previous decades of warfare suddenly became unnecessary. Many samurai became ronin or masterless samurai.

140. (B) European fighting men utilized gunpowder weapons increasingly by the Early Modern Era and this led to a similar decline in the power of the nobles and lords.

141. (D) With the advent of peace and stability, the samurai class lost their economic security, if not their official status.

142. (A) The Tokugawa shogunate was fearful of both a European takeover as had happened in the Philippines and also cultural influences such as Christianity, particularly Roman Catholic Christianity, which promoted loyalty to the European pope.

143. (B) With the exception of the Dutch trading at the port city of Nagasaki, the amount of knowledge of the world entering Japan was quite limited.

144. (C) Japan in the early seventeenth century began to severely restrict outside contact with the outside world. With the exception of diplomatic and trading missions occasionally by the Chinese and Koreans, only the Dutch were allowed to trade at the port of Nagasaki and then only one ship per year. The Spanish and Portuguese were not allowed upon pain of death.

145. (A) The Tokugawa shogunate heralded in a time of peace and stability despite being isolated largely from the world. Internally trade boomed and culture blossomed.

146. (B) The Pax Tokugawa was most similar to the Northern Renaissance in terms of its economic prosperity and cultural flowering.

147. (D) This situation symbolized Eastern control over Western influence, adding a touch of historical irony to its devastation in World War II.

148. (D) Strong centralized state structures, high population densities, and military sophistication enabled China and Japan in particular to set strict limits on Western contact in this time period.

149. (A) Only the Dutch, among Europeans, continued trade with Japan, although the English were allowed to trade but did not feel the small profits were worth the effort. It was primarily the Catholic powers, Spain and Portugal, that were forbidden to enter Japan.

150. (D) Europeans arrived in Japan during the wars for unification in the late 1500s and were valued for their gunpowder weapons. However, later when numbers of Japanese converted to Roman Catholicism Christianity, the Japanese shoguns were alarmed and this later led to tighter restrictions under the Tokugawa.

151. (B) The lines "To follow our nature is called the Way" is a clear reference to Chinese Daoism and, in fact, the world "Dao" translates to "the Way."

152. (C) Chinese influences in Vietnam shared a respect for education and the scholar-gentry class.

153. (A) Joint-stock companies such as the VOC or East India Company aggressively engaged in armed trading throughout the Indian Ocean and in Southeast Asia against both Muslim merchants and other European powers.

154. (D) Despite Confucian and Islamic influences, women in this region of the world maintained some status and independence.

155. (B) The sweet potato, an import from South America, was smuggled into China and later promoted by officials in Fujian province.

156. (B) New World foods into the Old World contributed to population increases in not only China but also areas like Ireland and Russia.

157. (D) Dutch Java became a prototype for European colonization of non-American lands.

158. (B) Landing in the islands, later named the Philippines, Magellan claimed them for Spain but was soon killed in a local conflict.

159. (D) Islamic calligraphy and minarets are well-known examples of Islamic design, and their presence indicates not a sharing of space between religions in this temple but a replacement.

160. (A) After the fall of the Ottoman Empire, Kemal Ataturk began a secularization program that had included the Hagia Sophia mosque and other landmarks such as the Ottoman palaces.

161. (A) Gunpowder weaponry and technology gave these states the military edge over their opposition.

162. (C) The Muslim Mughals, being in a minority, generally practiced toleration toward their Hindu subjects and cooperated with local Hindu Rajput rulers.

163. (C) Hinduism's popularity was based on its long existence, flexibility, appropriation of other faiths, and state support. Islam, while emphasizing charity, does not impose abolition of class or gender hierarchies.

164. (D) The Janissaries were an intriguing aspect of Ottoman rule. Similar to the Mamelukes in Egypt, they often achieved a level of social mobility but legally they were subject to the wishes of the Sultans.

165. (B) Young boys who were taken to serve the Ottoman state could be chosen for a number of positions in the devshirme system. Most famous role to be chosen was as Janissaries.

166. (A) Many young boys collected in the devshirme system later ended up serving the Ottoman states as court officials, Janissary generals, and in a few cases viziers. It was felt that the attainment of high positions would have helped their birth families.

167. (B) The Mughal Emperor Akbar was famous for his religious meetings in which clergy members of various faiths discussed spiritual matters.

168. (A) Akbar's descendant, Aurangzeb, was notorious for his reimposition of the non-believer tax and destroying Hindu temples.

169. (D) The Muslim Mughals were members of a minority faith in a sea of Hindus and other faiths such as Sikhs, Jains, and Parsis.

170. (B) The author of the Rotario mistook Hindus for Christians due to a lack of understanding. They had little knowledge of Hindus and Hinduism. However, they recognized almost immediately some local Muslims and attacked them.

171. (A) Since the Crusades, Europeans had long desired a route to Asia that was quicker and cheaper than the Silk Road route. With the monopolization of the Eurasian land and Mediterranean Sea route by Venetians and Ottomans, European sought an alternative route.

172. (C) The priest caste in Hindu society are known as the Brahmins while the other choices are all main castes in Hindu society.

173. (D) The Portuguese Age of Exploration in Asia resulted in only controlling port cities like Macao in China and Goa in India whereas the Spanish Age of Exploration resulted in the colonization of large areas in the Americas.

174. (C) The Islamic empires (Ottoman, Safavid, and Mughal) were also known as the "gunpowder" empires, which they used to gain and maintain control.

175. (A) All three "gunpowder" empires were ruled by warriors who adopted Islam but only the Safavid practiced Shi'a Islam.

176. (B) Phrases such as "I am neither in temple nor in mosque" and "Hindus and Muslims alike have achieved that End" demonstrate that the Bhakti movement was ecumenical in its attachments.

177. (A) Sikhism is a syncretic faith that blended aspects of Hinduism and Islam.

178. (A) The iconic Taj Mahal acted as a mausoleum and is now famed for its beauty and incorporation of Islamic design concepts.

179. (B) Monumental architecture such as palaces, castles, gardens, mausoleums, and even churches are meant to enhance a ruler's or a dynasty's stature.

180. (D) These patterns are each repeated and amplified as Western maritime empires move to the center of the world economy in the period 1450–1750, integrating the New World into the Old.

181. (D) Although Buddhism originated in the classical age of India and was heavily promoted by Asoka and other Mauryan emperors, some of its ideas had been borrowed by Hinduism and it spread to great effect throughout East Asia.

182. (A) Sikhism borrows monotheism from Islam and the ideas of reincarnation from Hinduism. It formed in the Punjab region of Northern India at the end of the 1400s.

183. (A) New World silver washed across the globe, upsetting regional economies in the sixteenth and seventeenth centuries.

184. (D) By 1750, each of the Muslim empires confronted a world situation where access to foreign trade involved well-armed Western intermediaries.

185. (A) Muslims, Chinese, Japanese, West Africans . . . political leaders in each region tended to ignore threats posed by rising Western power until it was too late and they had been forced into unfavorable trade relations.

186. (B) Akbar made efforts to reduce the hostility of the Hindu majority of the subcontinent to Muslim rule.

187. (B) Mongol expansion touched major civilizations across the Eurasian landmass, and its collapse opened space for the emergence of new powers, particularly in the Muslim world. Additionally, new Russian and Chinese ruling dynasties emerged in the period following Mongol rule.

188. (C) Awareness of this circumstance is key to understanding the move of the West toward the core of a new global economy in the period 1450–1750.

189. (D) Being the first to round the Cape of Good Hope and reach the Indian Ocean with the voyages of Vasco da Gama in 1495, the Portuguese followed up by seizing strategic positions at shipping choke points around the Indian Ocean basin soon thereafter.

190. (B) The fifteenth century saw an expansion of Europe to the Americas, Africa, and Asia. Merchants and missionaries used maritime trade winds to facilitate their travels to these parts of the world.

191. (C) The monsoons are seen as both a blessing and a curse since they enable agriculture to flourish yet also bring flooding.

192. (B) Muslims must pray towards the Holy City of Mecca five times a day, so knowledge of the correct direction is vital to the correct religious observance. It also helped with navigation and trade.

193. (B) In the Postclassical world, the most educated centers of learning were located in cities that were needed to support scholars who could devote themselves to study, learning, and teaching.

194. (D) The line "they had no knowledge whatever of such articles" indicates that this society was not connected with the larger Afro-Eurasian trade networks where spices and gold were highly valued. This was the same in the Americas. In fact, feathers from exotic birds were more highly prized than gold and silver.

195. (A) The Age of Discovery was motivated about finding an all-water route to Asia for cheaper trade goods to cut out the middle men in the Middle East and Mediterranean Sea.

196. (B) The trade in African slaves, European manufactured goods, and American crops dominated the trade relations in the Atlantic world in the Early Modern Era.

197. (B) The estimated mortality rate was 10 percent during the Middle Passage. This was certainly the most horrific part of the journey for these unfortunates.

198. (C) The Indian Ocean slave trade was smaller, but lasted longer and was less harsh than the Atlantic Slave trade.

199. (D) European firearms were superior to African weapons and highly sought after by Africans themselves.

200. (D) Northeast Africa is much closer to the Arab and Indian zones of the world economy than the Atlantic world. As for the other choices, ivory, gold, and domestic slaves were in demand around the Indian Ocean basin, and this trade was carried out by Muslim merchants who would have been the buyers of imported copies of the Koran.

201. (C) These Dutchmen came to be known as Boers (Dutch for "farmers"). Their descendants have been in South Africa for longer than most persons of European descent living in North America can claim to have been living here.

202. (D) In every other body of water listed, the West encountered existing naval and coastal military presences that required sustained campaigns to overcome or with whom Western ships had to coexist.

203. (A) The tribute such as caged exotic birds that can be seen at the bottom of the picture was a long-standing practice in Meso-American civilizations.

204. (C) Without Indian allies there were key moments in the battle of Tenochtitlan and at other times, where the European victory would have been lost.

205. (A) The merging of different religious aspects into one faith is common throughout world history. In the case of the Americas, it was inevitable that some aspects of Pre-Columbian faith would remain and be blended with the dominant faith of Christianity.

206. (B) The mountain above the Bolivian city of Potosi was responsible for an estimated 60% of the world's silver during the second half of the sixteenth century.

207. (A) Casta paintings reflect the rigid social class system that developed in Spanish colonial Americas.

208. (D) The conquest of the Americas and the Atlantic Slave Trade helped create Latin American society with its harsh inequalities. This in turn led to political insecurity and unrest.

209. (B) The Commercial Revolution intensified and greatly expanded world trade. The well-known Triangular Trade network was just one aspect of the Commercial Revolution.

210. (A) European nation-states' trade operated with mercantilist laws in order to increase their nation's wealth in relation to other nation-states. The sentence about subsidizing the slave traffic in order to stimulate sugar plantation economy demonstrates mercantilist thinking.

211. (B) While the sugar plantations of the Caribbean Island, taken together, made up the main destination of enslaved Africans, the sugar plantations of Brazil's Atlantic coast attracted more slave ships than any other single colony on its own. The British 13 colonies were never a major destination in the slave trade compared with points farther south.

212. (C) The early settlers of Massachusetts, the Puritans, were British citizens seeking greater religious freedom. We have no similar phenomenon in the settlement of Spanish Latin America, perhaps because religious minorities were effectively eliminated in a series of campaigns in Spain spanning from the Reconquista of 1492 when Jews and Muslims were expelled from Spain into the period of the Inquisition of the sixteenth and seventeenth centuries where Catholic orthodoxy was imposed by force on the population.

213. (B) This can be explained in large part by the near complete disappearance of the indigenous population of the New World in the face of smallpox and war.

214. (C) These estates were called encomiendas and were crucial to the establishment of an agricultural economy in the Spanish New World. "Bourbon reforms" were enacted to tighten royal control as the encomiendas began to form power bases to challenge the rule of the Spanish monarchy in the seventeenth and eighteenth centuries.

215. (D) Sugar, as in the Caribbean, was the initial generator of income in Brazil. Gold became important after its discovery in the Minas Gerais region.

216. (A) Polynesian settlement starting in the 1200s had a significant effect on the amount of tree cover in New Zealand.

217. (C) A subset of Austronesians who settled in the Pacific areas of New Zealand, Hawaiian islands, and Easter Island are called Polynesians.

218. (B) The use of architecture to lay out the vanishing lines of perspective is one of the essential elements that make this painting a masterpiece.

219. (A) The artist painted no religious figures despite depicting 21 individuals.

220. (A) Renaissance humanism promoted the use of vernacular languages.

221. (B) A marked increase in literacy due to the invention of movable type printing press led to later demands for literature and scripture in vernacular languages.

222. (B) The Northern Renaissance paintings were less religious than even Italian Renaissance paintings, which were less religious than European Medieval paintings.

223. (C) After the Black Death, the peasants were still tied to the land and had to fulfill certain feudal requirements but were increasingly part of the monied economy.

224. (D) Medieval and early modern European rulers, like rulers long before, them had a symbiotic relationship with religion and established belief systems.

225. (A) Johann Gutenberg's printing press spread Luther's ideas far and wide, and any attempt against him would have made him a martyr and maybe spread his ideas even farther.

226. (C) The scale and elaboration of monumental architecture is beyond their functionality and strongly reflects the government that orders or facilitates their construction. It nearly bankrupted the state because it was built to a scale to house many of the most powerful aristocrats in France so he could keep them in check.

227. (B) Building monumental architectural structures and controlling all aspects of government is indicative of an absolute monarch. Louis XIV was known as the "Sun King" since he was the center of the "French universe" reflecting the new knowledge of the era.

228. (A) Kings and their states with increasing taxation had the financial backing for supporting authors, artists, craftspeople, and explorers as well as scientists, all of whom increased the prestige and glory of the monarchs.

229. (D) Despite great cultural flowerings in both China and the Islamic Middle East, an orthodoxy had set in these societies and discouraged intellectual pursuits, which were seen as of little value. The ending of the voyages of the Chinese explorer Zheng He is a famous example.

230. (D) Luther's orientation toward biblical, as opposed to Catholic, authority makes his rejection of this element of Christian faith implausible.

231. (B) Other civilizations, as a rule, placed greater stock in religion, this being least true of the Chinese.

232. (D) Absolute monarchs, grown more rich and powerful through command of maritime trade and New World colonies, tended to centralize authority at the expense of the lesser aristocracy. The case of French monarchy and Louis XIV is a prime example.

233. (D) England stands apart from a trend toward absolute monarchy; patterns of limited monarchy dating back to the rise of Parliament in the twelfth century, and the Magna Carta of the thirteenth century, laid a basis for the emergence of a constitutional and not absolute monarchy in England.

234. (B) Ivan III was the first of the Russian leaders who refused to pay tribute to the Mongols and used the nascent Russian state to resist their domination.

235. (C) In the image above, one of the soldiers is clearly shown with an arquebus or early musket. Also, the reading mentions muskets.

236. (D) Russia's vast territories and undeveloped transportation network necessitated allowing the boyars great latitude in local affairs in return for allegiance and tax revenues.

237. (A) Russian serfs were ethnically the same as boyars, while the end of the Silk Road trade had no impact on serfdom, and Russia abhorred Mongol practices and customs.

238. (B) Czar Peter I was intent on a program of modernization, especially in shipbuilding for a modern navy, the construction of St. Petersburg which could act as a "window to the West," and controlling the boyars or nobles through the Tables or Ranks but he is also famously remembered for his opposition to the long beards which were symbols of Russian nobles.

239. (B) Throughout history, clothing and appearance have had symbolic importance. Sometimes they were seen as old fashioned or opposed to change whereas during the Ottoman era, the fez was seen as a more modern hat than turbans which were signs of status, towering, and time consuming to adorn.

240. (D) Regarding world trade, Russia played to its own strengths, supplying resources that its vast territory could produce in bulk.

241. (D) Referring to the previous question, the lands to the east of the Ural Mountains that were gained were vast and sparsely populated.

242. (A) Remember that St. Petersburg (Peter's town) is to the west of Moscow, a reminder of Peter the Great's general policy course.

243. (C) Monarchs, in general, were searching for paths to increased royal authority in the period after 1450. For Russia, westernization would serve that purpose.

244. (A) The goods listed on the left are in a raw or unfinished state while the goods on the right have been processed or handcrafted.

245. (D) The economic theory of mercantilism stipulates that colonies provide their mother-country with raw materials and in turn are provided with manufactured goods.

246. (B) Joint-stock companies such as the Dutch East India Company (VOC) and the British East India Company were the main engines for exploration, trade, and colonialism in the Early Modern Era.

247. (D) As the image shows, there are no ranks of oars for the Iberian ships who sailed the Atlantic Ocean as well as the Mediterranean Sea, which was where galleys with oars were primarily used.

248. (A) The Columbian Exchange dramatically increased contact between societies in the Eastern and Western Hemispheres. This included diseases, livestock, and crops.

249. (D) The line, established in 1493 in a treaty signed in the city of Tordesillas in Spain, passes through South America in a manner that roughly divides the present-day nation of Brazil from the Spanish-speaking portions of the continent. Even today, Portuguese is the official language in Brazil.

Chapter 3

250. (C) Traditional Chinese society, like most societies, was male dominated or patriarchal.

251. (D) Foot-binding was a traditional practice reaching back centuries in China. Its demise came about through a variety of factors but the arrival of the West played a key role, especially missionaries who sought to institute major changes in Chinese society.

252. (A) Korea, like other East Asian countries, were impressed by Western technology but were reflexively dismissive of the larger European culture.

253. (B) Yi Hangno used the phrase "the world is a big place" indicating that distance and geography in general kept these regions apart for much of history.

254. (A) The introduction of New World crops such as corn and sweet potatoes led to more food being produced. This was also helped by the intensification of farming on hillsides and in less settled areas like Szechuan province.

255. (B) The big increase in China's population and its interaction with the outside world led to a growing diaspora of Chinese outside the mainland. By 1911, there were Chinese communities scattered across the world.

256. (D) The Opium War highlighted the disparity in military superiority between China and the West. The Chinese forces were ineffective against British steam-powered warships with modern guns.

257. (A) Hong Kong remained British colony till 1997 and even today is governed under a different set of rules than the rest of China.

258. (B) The mid- to late nineteenth century saw a weakened China that was unable to control its own sovereignty. This period is what some Chinese call the "Century of Humiliations."

259. (A) The continent of Africa was divided up before, during, and after the Berlin Conference 1884–1885 in what was called the "Scramble for Africa."

260. (A) In the 1850s Japan opened up due to US Commodore Mathew Perry's visit and begun a series of reforms in foreign policy and trade.

261. (B) China enjoyed a favorable balance of trade during the Qing Dynasty all the way up until the advent of the opium trade in the early nineteenth century.

262. (B) Even in 1800, Chinese industrial capacity surpassed that of the British. For centuries the only commodity the British and other Westerners had that the Chinese desired was silver.

263. (D) This trend tends to breed resentment and poverty in the countryside, which can build to unsustainable levels and explode into revolt.

264. (C) This imperial arrogance causes a stunning lack of awareness of the danger the West would pose.

265. (B) The port at Nagasaki was open for trade and ships from China, Korea, and Holland were allowed to enter. So called "Dutch Learning" was steadily entering Japan and translated. Its dissemination, however, was limited.

266. (C) East Asian nations believed that their cultures were vastly superior to Western but were interested in European science and technology, especially military.

267. (C) Since Japan was largely closed off for many years, information about the actual governing of the nation was very limited.

268. (A) Commodore Perry's mission was a major turning point in Japanese history and brought many profound changes to the nation and the world.

269. (B) The closure of Japan came to an abrupt end soon after Perry's visit in 1853 and would soon provide an impetus for the modernizing reforms under the emperor Meiji.

270. (A) Japan's changes in the Meiji era are often compared to the lack of reforms in China during the same period. The 100 Days of Reform are a point in fact.

271. (D) Historians now challenge the idea of Japanese modernization as a direct result of the arrival of the Americans. Many of the precursors of modernization were already in place in Tokugawa Japan.

272. (D) Industrialization of the textile industry used female labor largely due their low salaries and the belief in appropriate types of industries for females.

273. (B) Since this individual is from a rural area and a member of the Buddhist clergy, he would most likely be sympathetic to the plight of the young women, which would make him a reliable source for a historian studying this period.

274. (C) Commodore Mathew Perry's ships arrived in Tokyo Bay in 1853 and demonstrated their weapons. Witnessing this, Japan opened to Western trade soon thereafter.

275. (C) Much like the British monarch, the Meiji emperor was more or less a figurehead leader.

276. (A) Western models proceeded on more of a free enterprise or laissez-faire footing while Russia and Japan were more state-directed.

277. (B) Religious westernization would have meant conversion to Christianity, Shinto remained the state religion and together with Buddhism maintained mass followings.

278. (A) As was common during the second wave of imperialism, local customs, dress, and hairstyles were slow to change.

279. (B) The scene in the newspaper would be a common one in Asian ports in this time period as Asia and many other parts of the world were incorporated into the economy of the world.

280. (C) "Divide and conquer" remained a key tactic of control for colonial powers since the Dutch pioneered it in seventeenth-century Java.

281. (A) Napoleon's invasion, though ultimately a failure started a process where Egypt's fate was moving away from under Ottoman control.

282. (C) The accidental discovery by a French officer in Napoleon's army opened up hieroglyphics that had been indecipherable for centuries.

283. (C) In Islamic Sunni tradition the human figure is never depicted and any image of the prophet Muhammad or of Allah is considered highly disrespectful. In Shi'a Islam, depicting the human form is allowed as in the case of Persian miniatures.

284. (D) The introduction of the printing press by Napoleon's army into Egypt in 1798 would challenge both the monopoly of the scribes on the written word and the Sultanate's control over information.

285. (A) Turkish Muslims were officially the elite due to their religion and language but social realities tested this status. Many Christian and Jewish Ottomans were able to use their connections to take advantage of the burgeoning trade.

286. (B) Similar to efforts in Japan, Russia, and China, the Ottoman Empire made efforts to adapt to changes in the world, especially their apparent weakness relative to the West.

287. (D) The Ottoman's poor performance during the Crimean War and the increased exposure to Western powers encouraged the Ottomans to reform.

288. (B) The Tanzimat Reforms from the 1830s to 1870s removed the legal inequality against Christians and Jews and other minorities. These were part of modernization efforts after Ottoman losses in the Crimean War.

289. (A) Subject peoples such as Slavs and Arabs demanded more autonomy and even independence. This was part of a global process of rising nationalism in the nineteenth century.

290. (D) This question serves as a useful listing of the Tanzimat reforms.

291. (C) Muhammad Ali's Egypt stands as a case of thwarted industrialization outside the West, contrasting with successful industrialization in Japan and Russia.

292. (D) This waterway was a hugely important shortcut around the African landmass.

293. (C) Yet, by 1914 neither would be formally colonized but both would be reduced to economically dependent relationships with the West.

294. (C) The Great Game was about territorial claims and strategic advantage in Central Asia between the Russian and the British empires. It was the backdrop for the famous novel, *Kim* by Rudyard Kipling.

295. (A) The Great Game where Britain and Russia competed for control over Central Asia was very similar to European competition for colonies in Africa.

296. (B) The Seven Years War, was a global conflict fought in India as well as North America, the Caribbean, and Europe. Through the British East India Company as an arm of the British government will now be unchallenged on the Indian subcontinent.

297. (B) The British East India Company with the help of native forces or sepoys defeated the French in a decisive battle at Plessy in 1757. This battle was part of a larger contest that is known in world history as the Seven Years War or in America as the French and Indian War.

298. (A) The use of the phrase "Firmly relying ourselves on the truth of Christianity" shows the arrogance of the conquerors. This assumption and others like it will later grate on Indian sensibilities.

299. (C) The British East India company was increasingly seen as insensitive toward Indian belief systems. The most notorious example of this involved a new type of rifle that used animal grease (reportedly from pork or beef fat) to insert the cartridge down the barrel. This helped cause the Sepoy Mutiny or Uprising.

300. (B) A shift starting in the 1830s and increasing after the Sepoy Rebellion moved the British away from working with locals to one of paternalistic rule over inferior natives.

301. (C) Mercantilist thought ordained that colonies like India should benefit their mother countries and this ideology remained strong even when more capitalists and laissez-faire attitudes became popular in Britain.

302. (C) The fact that the speaker spoke in London and presumably in the English language shows that he was British educated and had the means to travel such a distance. This group was fostered in colonial societies and was essential to the smooth running of the colonial venture.

303. (D) All of the choices capture the mix of divide and conquer, paternalism, and racism that characterized the colonial relationship.

304. (A) A marked increase in women and children joining their European family members who were stationed in Asian colonies took place increasingly in the nineteenth century as transportation and health services improved.

305. (C) In the seventeenth and eighteenth centuries about one-quarter to one-third of Europeans died after two years due to disease. By the nineteenth century the number had fallen considerably and with improved transportation, it was common for women and even children to join their family members.

306. (C) The role of the colony in the industrial era is not to be a center of industrial production.

307. (B) Colonial society functioned best when each person knew his or her "place." Traditional hierarchical structures assisted in this arrangement.

308. (B) Ritual wife burning was targeted by British colonial officials as a barbaric practice that must be brought to a stop.

309. (B) Loyal cooperation was more valued than coerced obedience when it came to regents who were often trusted with important administrative tasks.

310. (A) The early membership of the Congress Party was made up of the middle class professionals. Gandhi will later transform it into a mass-movement.

311. (B) Of the reasons listed, it was primarily European susceptibility to African diseases kept Europeans out of the interior of Africa.

312. (C) The Journey to the Coast was often as deadly for the enslaved Africans as the more notorious Middle Passage but we have few records of such losses.

313. (D) This famous image of slave ships brought home to many people the inhumane conditions associated with the trade in human beings.

314. (B) Slavery in the Atlantic world came to an end in the nineteenth century as a result of the abolition movement.

315. (A) Despite Laird's statements about moral superiority, he was closer to the true causes of British exploration when he spoke of the steam engine.

316. (B) Laird's statements are almost a textbook definition of Social Darwinism with his assumptions of white superiority and the "dark corners" of Africa.

317. (D) The Berlin Conference in 1884 was an attempt to bring order to the Scramble for Africa and avoid hostilities between European powers.

318. (C) African representatives were notoriously not invited to Berlin. Furthermore, borders between African colonies and later nations would disregard ethnic and linguistic group territories.

319. (B) European powers built railroad and other infrastructures for their own benefit. Despite the new capitalist ideology, they still adhered to the idea that colonies existed for the benefit of the mother-countries.

320. (A) Social Darwinism proposed the idea that the more powerful nations had a "right" to exploit weaker ones.

321. (B) New World crops such as corn and manioc led to population increase as it had done in many other parts of the world.

322. (B) Particularly racist notions about the African inability to learn, notoriously prevalent in Belgian rule of the Congo for instance, meant that colonial administrations viewed setting up anything more than rudimentary schooling as a waste of time and resources. Church groups did it out of charity if any Westerners bothered to set up schools at all.

323. (D) Famously, no Africans were involved in negotiations that, to a large degree, drew political boundaries that remain in place on the continent today.

324. (D) To oversimplify, Spencer can be viewed perhaps as combining the conclusions of Thomas Hobbes (life is "a war of each against all") and Charles Darwin (natural selection) to come to the conclusion that "survival of the fittest" was the proper state for human affairs.

325. (A) European nation-states' trade operated with mercantilist laws in order to increase their nation's wealth in relation to other nation-states.

326. (C) The American colonies were long upset with mercantilist ideas and practices. The famous Boston Tea Party was one such demonstration of their anger.

327. (D) Many French soldiers were demoralized by both the conditions of fighting in Haiti with its high death toll due to disease plus the contradiction of their goals in Haiti with Republican ideals that they had been raised on

328. (D) The British antislavery movement was just beginning in the 1780s and had not had much influence beyond England and the newly freed American colonies.

329. (B) Latin America had weak political institutions such as independent courts and a lack of universal suffrage. This continued into the twentieth century up until the 1980s.

330. (D) The wars of Independence were not social revolutions and this stifled political ambitions of the non-Creole majority. This combined with the infighting among the Creoles produced numerous revolutions and coup d'etats.

331. (C) The viewpoint of the Qing government toward the so-called "coolies" did not discourage them from migrating in search of better opportunities.

332. (A) The sale of guano mirrors other Latin American exports like tin, copper, sugar, bananas, and coffee in that they are for export to Europe and North America and have contributed, some say to a "neocolonialist" relationship with the world economy.

333. (A) Interdependence means a dependence of two or more things on one another, this was definitely increasingly the case of the world economy in the nineteenth century. It is also related to the idea of globalization which is not a twenty-first-century phenomenon.

334. (B) The Diaz regime (1876–1911) oversaw many improvements in Mexico but these were limited to urban areas, involved crony capitalism and foreign domination of some industries, like oil production.

335. (D) While there were clear gains during the Porferio era, the advancement of democracy was not one of them.

336. (D) Creole elites aimed for little more change than ejection of the peninsulares; Haiti's revolution showed the risks of slave uprisings for the Creole elites.

337. (C) The year 1800 is a good, round year to imagine the Industrial Revolution gaining real momentum. Patterns of urbanization, factory work, and other items that we recognize to be "industrial" became increasingly prominent after that date.

338. (C) These men were known as caudillos, and their interference in politics has become such a pattern that historians speak of a "caudillo phenomenon" in Latin American history.

339. (D) Southern Europeans, Italians in particular, were attracted to Argentina in the decades before and after the turn of the twentieth century—a period of massive emigration to the United States as well. Inexpensive steam ship passage was key.

340. (B) Latin American nations serve as something of a preview of the challenges of post-colonial development the rest of the developing world would face in the post–World War II era. Economic dependency on the West was chief among those challenges.

341. (C) Western sailors and missionaries brought the first deadly diseases to the Hawaiian islands and the population was nearly halved within decades.

342. (B) The geographic isolation of indigenous peoples left them (especially their immune systems) unprepared for the onslaught of Western intrusion into their lands.

343. (A) Inequality among the different social classes in France is considered to be one of the main causes leading to the Revolution in 1789.

344. (C) Within the Third Estate (bourgeoisie, peasants, and urban poor), only the bourgeoisie's condition was improved by the French Revolution and Napoleonic reforms.

345. (A) Adam Smith's seminal work observed factory conditions where changes in production in a pin factory increased output.

346. (B) The division of labor was a key component for the industrialization since it sped up the manufacturing process and led to greater output.

347. (A) The Scientific Revolution led to the Industrial Revolution by the practical application of science in technology.

348. (C) Britain had the right geography, government support, and infrastructure to encourage industrialization. It also had the right social conditions in a middle class that sought opportunities in industrialization.

349. (A) As machines got too big to be accommodated inside houses, factories were built to handle their large sizes. Also, as demand increased for more labor, workers were not part of family units.

350. (C) With the invention of the machines that were not dependent on water or wind, factories were moved to the cities, hence urbanization.

351. (D) Smiles' use of terms like "over-government" and phrases like "Heaven helps those who help themselves" clearly show his view in the debate about government's role in helping the less fortunate.

352. (C) The new capitalist class promoted the values of laissez-faire and minimal government involvement in the economy. The old paternal yet condescending attitude of the landed class slowly gave way.

353. (A) The unemployment created by the invention of labor-saving machines led some workers to take out their frustrations on the machines and those who owned them.

354. (C) Karl Marx saw history as a constant struggle between the "haves and have nots." He predicted that workers would overthrow the bourgeoisie and create a worker-run state.

355. (B) Germany entered the race for overseas empire later than other nations and felt overshadowed by Britain's large navy.

356. (A) Social Darwinism was a popular concept in the nineteenth century and was used to justify imperialism. They added to and/or replaced other beliefs such as religious bigotry that were more common in earlier eras.

357. (D) When you hear or see the word *industrial*, think of the word *factory*. All of the other choices were preindustrial motives as well.

358. (C) Initial industrialization is often of the "light industrial" variety, focused around textile production. This is greatly different from what industrialization was to become.

359. (D) With the revolution starting in Great Britain, it makes sense that it would spread to continental Europe and then the United States.

360. (C) The 1830s saw the Reform Bill in England and Jacksonian democracy in the United States, where voting rights were expanded to new segments of the population.

361. (A) The 13 colonies cannot be said to have contained a "peasantry" on anything like the feudal terms that existed in France, while statements I and II were true for both.

362. (B) Russian serfdom lasted decades or even centuries longer than in the rest of Europe. It was widely held to be an anachronism, even in Russia in the decades preceding its abolition.

363. (A) Historians argue that its late industrialization and small middle class, widespread illiteracy and poor performance in the Crimean War and later Russo-Japanese war were a result of the long history of serfdom.

364. (D) Russia was intent on being an industrial power and that required goods that could be bought and used for industrial and business users.

365. (B) Russia's industrialization program was impressive but its late entry meant it was far behind other nations. It will not be until the 1940s in World War II that Russian Industrial output reached Western levels.

366. (D) The assassination of Czar Alexander II in 1881 led to a wave of repression against suspected radicals and non-Russians like Jews. It was felt that non-Russians were a threat to the state. This was part of a pattern throughout Russian history and continued even into the Communist era.

367. (B) Many Jews fled the Russian empire, and America was a preferred destination, particularly through Ellis Island in New York. This was one of the great diasporas and had profound implications for world history.

368. (B) Both managed to imitate Western developments while maintaining distinctive characteristics.

369. (D) Remember that the choice must be incorrect. Czarist rule was highly autocratic and spawned multiple uprisings against it from the 1825 Decembrist uprising to anarchist plots of the 1880s to the 1905 Revolution and the revolutions of 1917.

370. (B) The Crimea is a peninsula protruding down from Ukraine into the Black Sea, it is so warm there it has been a summer vacation spot for centuries.

371. (C) The Jesuit priest Malagrida (which is most likely a pen name) speaks of "abominable sins," and "sinful ways" of city's residents. Choices (A) and (B) refer to more physical forces.

372. (B) Immanuel Kant proposed that the earthquakes and other volcanic activity tended to occur during the autumn season. While incorrect, he was one of the first thinkers to propose a physical explanation, rather than a moral one.

373. (B) The modern world is largely based on the application of science and logic to understand our world and sometimes create solutions for problems.

374. (C) The British East India Company and other joint-stock companies brought many previously isolated areas of the world into one global economic system.

375. (A) This painting has an interesting composition with divide between East and West, the top and bottom and the light and dark halves. Its location in the British East India Company headquarters presents an extremely benign view of the company's activities.

376. (D) The British East India Company, along with the Dutch East India Company (VOC), was one of the first international companies and ended up being involved in numerous incidents as a semi-branch of British foreign policy. It was not however involved in the Congress of Vienna, which was a diplomatic endeavor.

Chapter 4

377. (A) By 1900, China was in danger of being carved up the way Africa was during the Congress of Berlin in 1884. The defeat of China in the Boxer Rebellion soon led to competing territorial claims by outside powers.

378. (A) A weakened China after the Boxer Rebellion almost immediately became prey for foreign powers, and the competition among them soon led to hostility and war.

379. **(C)** Students were the most active groups in both events in Chinese history. It's interesting that the call for democracy and other reforms were among their demands.

380. **(B)** When the provisions of the Versailles Treaty became known in China, students and intellectuals erupted in anger that endangered the life of some members of their diplomatic delegation.

381. **(A)** Efforts by educated Chinese and western missionaries since the late nineteenth century had begun to reduce the practice of foot-binding by 1919.

382. **(D)** Karl Marx theorized that in an industrial society the workers or proletariat would eventually rise up and overthrow the capitalist or bourgeoisie class. Mao saw the revolutionary potential in the peasant class. This is known as Maoism.

383. **(B)** Mao believed that the landlord class would have to be eliminated throughout China and that violence was necessary.

384. **(B)** Both the Soviet Union and Mao's China used the Soviet Realism style in its propaganda posters. This encouragement of women was consistent with the communist ideology that stressed equality.

385. **(D)** As we have seen throughout world history, women's struggle has been an uphill battle and no less so in Communist-leaning nations. Still, the gains made by Chinese women within three generations were remarkable.

386. **(B)** While the Chinese nationalists never fully suspended offensive operations against communist base areas or suspected communist sympathizers between 1927 and the communist victory in 1949, the period after Japan's all-out invasion of China in 1937 prompted some cessation of hostilities between nationalists and communists in pursuit of the common aim of defeating Japanese aggression.

387. **(A)** This campaign coincided with drought and crop failures that led to widespread food shortages.

388. **(C)** Significant institutional and economic disruption resulted from this campaign that was both launched and dismantled by Mao.

389. **(A)** Since Deng Xiaoping became leader of the Chinese Communist Party in 1979, China has seen economic but not political reform.

390. **(A)** The image above which shows a strong Russian sailor and ship delivering a devastating blow to stereotypically-drawn Japanese sailor and ship was typical of European propaganda before this conflict. The impact of the Japanese defeat on Russia would be one of the world's histories great upsets and both give encouragement to non-Europeans all over the world and be a harbinger for World War II in Asia.

391. **(C)** This shows the weakened state of China by 1904 that major powers were fighting over its territory and they could just look on helplessly.

392. (C) The depiction of the methods and weapons of war shows a clear militaristic bent, that was all too common at the time in the world.

393. (A) Due to increased world trade and economic integration, the effects of the Great Depression were felt around the world and not just in America and Europe.

394. (A) The Pacific theater required land, air, and sea forces due to the many islands, archipelagos, and mainland campaigns.

395. (C) The topography of South East Asia and the Pacific Islands is largely made up of rainforest or jungle conditions and was challenging for United States and Allied soldiers.

396. (B) Propaganda and censorship were the norm during wartime even for democracies. A photo such as this was feared for its depiction of dead United States forces, which might diminish public support for the war.

397. (D) Fascism involves very tight government supervision of not only the political but also the economic life of a nation. Laissez-faire means just the opposite.

398. (C) Japan's more homogeneous ethnic makeup made events like Kristallnacht (Crystal Night/Night of the Broken Glass), an anti-Jewish movement, a nonissue there.

399. (D) Japanese workers are unionized but generally do not strike. They traditionally enjoy lifetime employment at a single firm in a broad social agreement that more or less has maintained labor peace.

400. (C) Following World War II with its inclusion of a "no war" clause into its constitution, Japan does not engage in aggressive actions and only maintains a small armed force for defensive purposes only.

401. (A) Since 1949, the United States followed a policy of containment of communism and that was the prime rationale for America's involvement in the Korean War. This idea would later be expanded to the so-called "domino theory," which saw communism expanding all over Asia if it was not checked.

402. (C) At Yalta agreement in 1945, the Allies agreed to the division of both Germany and Korea with much less thought given to the latter.

403. (A) Vietnamese nationalists under Ho Chi Minh hoped to avoid a conflict with both the French and Americans after the war was over. The wording of the document was deliberately chosen for that purpose.

404. (C) The opening of the Declaration with the lines "All men are created equal. They are endowed by their Creator with certain inalienable rights; among these are Life, Liberty, and the pursuit of Happiness" shows a clear influence of the Enlightenment and specifically the American experience of an independence struggle.

405. (D) As industrialization became state policy in many Asian nations, it drew workers from the agricultural sector, which was also being mechanized.

406. (B) Following a Japan as a model, many Asian nations began to focus on an export driven economic. These nations became known as the Asian Tigers or Tiger Cubs.

407. (C) Indonesia, Thailand, and Malaysia are all nations in South East Asia and these nations have been referred to as the "Tiger Cubs."

408. (C) The rise of fascism and Nazi aggression in Europe had a profound impact on the security of Jewish life. However, strict immigration laws closed off many avenues for fleeing Jews. Many chose British-controlled Palestine, which was also illegal, but there were strong historic ties to the Holy Land.

409. (A) The two competing yet justifiable claims by Israelis and Palestinians make this conflict one of the most intractable in the world today.

410. (A) The Mandate system was established after the Versailles treaty and based on the secret wartime agreement, the notorious Sykes-Picot negotiations in 1916.

411. (B) The Arab revolt against the Ottomans was encouraged by Britain, through their officer on the ground, the famous Lawrence of Arabia. The Arabs were promised self-rule in the Husain-McMahon correspondence.

412. (D) The Morgenthau memoirs remain a powerful indictment against Turkey for its denial of culpability for the genocidal acts committed by the Turkish government during World War I. At the time, the United States was not at war against the Ottomans and had little reason to lie or exaggerate.

413. (C) Rising nationalism led to a push for many groups to establish ethnic states out of the Ottoman Empire. By 1915, groups such as the Greeks, Serbs, Romanians, and Bulgarians had already broken away to form new nations.

414. (A) The current policy of the Turkish government was that there was no plan of extermination of Armenians and any killings that took place are an unfortunate part of the messiness of war and were in fact the acts of bandits and not government policy.

415. (B) With no history of secular government, Middle Easterners have struggled with Islam's correct role in Middle East state and society to this very day.

416. (C) In the mid-twentieth century, the driving force in the Middle East was nationalism and this is clear in the reading. However, by the 1970s, Islamist forces like the Muslim Brotherhood and the Iranian Revolution were challenging secular governments across the Middle East.

417. (D) This United Nations resolution was adopted unanimously by the UN Security Council on November 22, 1967, in the aftermath of the Six-Day War. It has remained the basis for peace talks ever since and was adopted by the Palestinian people.

418. (C) The conflict in the Holy Land has changed over the years from 1967 with no signs of ending but switching from periods of crisis to periods of relative calm.

419. (A) This support came to be known as the Balfour Declaration.

420. (D) Egypt, like the rest of Africa, still imports most of its durable consumer goods.

421. (C) The mere fact that the West did not have an influence on events makes the Iranian Revolution unique in twentieth-century history.

422. (C) The Organization of Petroleum Exporting Countries (OPEC) fixes oil prices at levels agreed on by the governments of developing countries, not Western consumers.

423. (D) The invasion ultimately destabilizes the nation, which will later lead to the rise of the Taliban with its strict observance of Islam.

424. (C) The geography is Afghanistan is almost the opposite of Vietnam in that it is very dry, has sparse vegetation, and in a high altitude.

425. (B) Indian nationalists like Nehru never failed to point out the negative effects of British rule and even nonpartisan Indian thinkers like Mukerjee mention the massive unemployment of a traditional Indian industry.

426. (D) The forced integration of formally isolated economies like Japan or semi-isolated economies like India often had negative local consequences. This could be called an earlier wave of globalization.

427. (C) Gandhi's Salt March in 1930 is a famous example of a colonized people strenuously resisting a colonial power yet not resorting to physical violence.

428. (A) British military officers were opposed to yielding any colony back to the colonized subject peoples.

429. (B) The movement of people after the partition of India was one of the largest migrations in world history.

430. (B) The violence of the partition of India and Pakistan had long-term causes dating back to the period of British colonial rule and further back to Hindu resentment of Muslim domination in the Mughal era.

431. (D) Through the use of science and technology, technocrats and scientists sought to increase the food supply.

432. (C) India's vibrant democracy has had many problems but they have been successful in averting famines.

433. (C) The Bangladeshi Nationalist program was rejected by the West Pakistani's thereby initiating a crisis that later led to the partition of Pakistan.

434. (B) Pakistan was founded as a state for Muslims albeit in two halves. But making Urdu the only official language and other issues caused the Bengalis to chafe under West Pakistani control.

435. (D) Caste remains a defining feature of Indian civilization despite decades of (perhaps half-hearted) government efforts to reform it out of existence.

436. (B) With the exception of a few areas such as Ethiopia and Liberia, Africa was under the control of European powered since the nineteenth century.

437. (C) Postal systems, like other aspects of modernity, were established in the twentieth century.

438. (A) World War II forever changed the relationship between colonizer and colonized, especially in Africa. Decolonization was largely inevitable.

439. (C) By the early 1960s, most nations in Africa were free of European rule. It was overwhelmingly a peaceful transition with the exception of nations like Kenya and Rhodesia (Zimbabwe).

440. (B) Apartheid is the Afrikaner word for the South African policy of strict racial segregation that existed from 1948 to the 1990s.

441. (B) South Africa's apartheid regime was based on a stricter implementation of laws that harkened back to ideas of social Darwinism and scientific racism from the colonial era.

442. (D) South Africa ended its Apartheid regime in the early 1990s and when it held elections, Nelson Mandela was elected president of the nation, traveling the common road of "prisoner to president" in decolonization.

443. (C) The Nationalist Party that negotiated independence in 1960 ruled an apartheid state where the majority black population could not vote.

444. (B) Most developing nations have experienced military rule at some point.

445. (D) Nigeria's petroleum industry is the main force behind its GDP.

446. (D) European settler minorities had lived in the colonies for generations by the 1960s, occupied high rank in society, and were numerous enough to marshal the resources to put up stiff resistance to decolonization.

447. (B) The mention of the employment in the Americas and the revolutionary violence in Europe were clear factors that promoted migration to the Americas.

448. (B) The image shows a strong stream from the Iberian nations of Spain and Portugal. The latter was a Portuguese colony for centuries.

449. (C) Since the Monroe Doctrine, Latin American nations have had to navigate their relationships with the United States through difficult times, especially during the Cold War era.

450. (B) The United States maintained an isolationist policy in Europe but was quite interventionist in the Americas and Asia. Understanding the friction that the interventions caused, President Roosevelt promoted the "Good Neighbor" policy toward Latin America.

451. (A) The poverty and inequality of prerevolutionary Mexican was the main cause of the revolt and kept it going for 10 long years.

452. (B) Foreign-controlled companies owned by Americans in Mexico or the British in China caused a groundswell of antiforeign sentiment that were one of the main causes of the revolutions in those countries in 1910.

453. (D) When France and the Low Countries fell to the Nazi blitzkrieg, Britain was said to have "stood alone." This claim is only partly true in that it had many parts of the empire behind it as well and many nations contributed armed forces and volunteers.

454. (B) The war against fascism immediately brought up the irony of nonwhite peoples fighting for imperialist states like Britain and France.

455. (C) They serve as a preview for the challenges of postcolonial development in a world economy with the West at its economic core.

456. (D) Cuba's colonial heritage left it overly dependent on sugar production. The United States imposed a blockade of trade with Cuba soon after 1959, leaving Cuba with few trading partners but the Soviets. Since the 1990 collapse of the USSR, Cuba has struggled for economic growth in the context of this blockade.

457. (B) The pattern of migration to the cities is, perhaps, surprising to North Americans, but true. This shows the impact of the media on one's views.

458. (B) Statement III ruins choices (C) and (D) since colonialism ended in the nineteenth century. Both I and II are accurate as the world witnessed the collapse of the Chilean copper industry and the rise of corporatist dictatorial regimes (such as the Vargas regime in Brazil and the Peron regime in Argentina).

459. (C) The introduction of nonindigenous species into previously isolated regions can damage those areas forever.

460. (A) Australia's rabbit-proof fence, the Great Wall of China, the Berlin Wall—these types of barriers seem expedient at the time to some but rarely fulfill their promise.

461. (A) Indian troops as well as African, Australian, New Zealand, Canadian, West Indian, and Irish troops joined the British side during World War I.

462. (B) Trench warfare was generally a static form of warfare compared to World War II, which saw blitzkrieg attacks by German forces and surprise attacks by the Japanese.

463. (B) World War I and other total wars involved the mobilization of all resources as well as public opinion, which can both be seen in the poster.

464. (C) Women's heavy participation in World War I was seen as justification for women's suffrage in many Western nations.

465. (B) Yeats wrote this poem with the postwar unrest in mind, especially in Russia, Germany, and his native Ireland.

466. (D) In nations like Germany, Austria-Hungary, Russia, and the Ottoman Empire their monarchs were forced to abdicate.

467. (B) Fascism promotes imperialist aggression as good for the nation in terms of power but also for the benefit of the people's "vitality."

468. (C) This easy question asks students to find the commonalities in the Interwar Era.

469. (C) As part of the Versailles treaty strict limits were placed Germany's armed forces. They were not allowed to have an air force or tanks and their navy and size of the army was severely shrunk as can be seen in the chart as well as the graphics on the map.

470. (D) It is widely argued that punishing Germany helped Adolf Hitler and the Nazis rise to power. Although the treaty was unpopular with most Germans the propaganda value of Germany's victimhood helped them win the elections of 1933.

471. (C) Studying the dates and noticing trends are important in answering this question.

472. (C) The Allies made Germany pay financially, territorially, and in other ways for World War I and this weakened its economy.

473. (B) The fall of the Berlin Wall in 1989 heralded the end of communism in Eastern Europe and a de-escalation of tensions between America and the Soviet Union. The USSR ended within two years in 1991.

474. (C) United States President John F. Kennedy's famous speech takes strong issue with the idea of a wall to keep East Berliners trapped behind the Iron Curtain and helped it become an iconic symbol of communist oppression.

475. (B) The United States wanted to have a strong trading partner and Cold War concerns were important as well in the plans to rebuild Europe.

476. (C) Understanding the insidious impact of the Great Depression on European political life, the United States was concerned about economic recovery, especially in light of the looming Cold War.

477. (B) This advantage of colonial holdings was established during late-nineteenth-century economic downturns.

478. (B) Be careful not to be too quick to pick choice (A). European elites, particularly Central and Eastern European elites, were traumatized by the Bolshevik seizure of power in Russia, and the first promise of fascist regimes wherever they came to power was to stamp out the communist threat.

479. (D) These Cold War–era military alliances faced each other across a dividing line that Winston Churchill famously termed the Iron Curtain. For many decades World War III was expected to be fought between these two alliances.

480. (B) By the 1960s Western elites and general populations both accepted decolonization as something of an inevitability; France stands as something of an exception, fighting two bitter wars to maintain colonial holdings, one in Indonesia and the other in Algeria. Statement III is nonetheless mainly false.

481. (C) In late 1917, Russia was rocked by a second revolution, this time by Bolsheviks, a radical group of communists under their leader Vladimir Lenin.

482. (B) Some historians place 1917 as the start of the Cold War due to the radical economic policies advocated by Russian communists. However, other scholars see the start as events in World War II such as the Yalta Agreement or Red Army liberation of Eastern Europe.

483. (A) The Great Ukrainian Famine (1932–1933) or the Holodomor is seen by many people as a man-made disaster and an attack on the Ukrainian people.

484. (C) Stalin's collectivization removed any personal initiative for Russian peasants to grow more crops. Coupled with the sale of grain to pay for the industrialization and anti-Ukrainian feeling, these factors all led to a severe shortage of food.

485. (C) According to some scholars, a continuity in Russian history is a xenophobic attitude toward foreign ideas and fear of foreign invasion.

486. (B) There are numerous causes of the Cold War, including geopolitical leaders' personalities and overreactions to escalating events. However, probably the most common explanation is ideological, which can be argued began in 1917.

487. (A) The Soviet regime forcibly imposed collective farming, which alienated some prosperous farmers, the so-called kulaks. These enemies were then eliminated in the anti-kulak campaigns.

488. (D) Stalin's persecution of so-called "kulaks" or well-off peasants mirrored the actions of other totalitarian regimes like Nazi Germany, fascist Italy, or Khmer Rouges' Cambodia.

489. (B) Throughout the communist world, basic goods were kept within reach of the working classes and peasantry. This helps to explain the popularity of these regimes, particularly in Cuba.

490. (A) By the 1970s, the economic problems in the USSR were hard to ignore, and the premier Mikhail Gorbachev attempted to reform the system.

491. (C) Both regimes are considered to be totalitarian in that their areas of control over the populace were vast and unprecedented.

492. (D) Soviet development (as with many developments until recent decades) is not known for environmental concern.

493. (D) Josip Tito's Yugoslavia mounted a more or less independent resistance to Nazi invasion during World War II, liberated itself from fascist occupation, and emerged as an independent socialist state after World War II.

494. (A) Vast resources inside the USSR, plus access to that of satellite Eastern European nations, make statement III untrue. Since both statements I and II are true, choice (A) is best.

495. (C) Glasnost is a Russian term for the economic reforms that allowed for more private ownership, and perestroika translates to a new "openness" in politics that allowed for more public criticism of Soviet government and society. Soviet socialism could not survive more than five or six years of these policies.

496. (B) Lyrics "Oppenheimer's deadly toy" and "winnable war" is a clear reference to the competition in both conventional and nuclear arms that the United States and the Soviet Union engages in during the Postwar Era.

497. (C) MAD is an acronym that is used frequently to describe the Cold War. It is based on the theory of deterrence, which holds that the threat of using strong weapons against the enemy prevents the enemy's use of those same weapons.

498. (B) After World War II, many people were alarmed at the rising populations in the developing world. This rehashing of Thomas Malthus's ideas of overpopulation combined with Cold War fears of communism taking hold among poor peoples, resulted in attempts to boost agricultural efficiency.

499. (B) Liberal democracy fell in Russia, Germany, Italy, and across Eastern Europe in the period between the world wars, appearing to be a failed political arrangement to many. Its resurgence after World War II was reinforced by the emergence of the United States as a superpower.

500. (C) Central America, including Mexico, is regarded as part of the North American continent, and NAFTA, short for the North American Free Trade Agreement, was signed in 1994 under the Clinton administration.